There really is no greater place
on earth. Just ask a white American.
More than a country America
has travelled the world like an idea
virus with Coca-Cola, Action Movies
and drone attacks as its symptoms.
Existing in a state of middle finger
raised, willful ignorance where
book-learning, science, facts, understanding
and awareness are viewed by most
Americans as gay and weak. America
is a place of extreme juxtapostion
and hypocrisy. They spout freedom
and live in fear, they preach equality
and strive for a white mans Utopia
an- apartheid built by wealth and
corporate sponsored government.
They gun each other down at
staggering rates, worship the least
among them and eat a ~~ste~~ plate
full of death three times a day...
And I would do pretty much anything
to get a green card.
The place is fucking awesome.

Alabama. It's easy to think of New York or Los Angeles when one thinks of America but that's not her. It's best to think of America as Alabama. A place filled with Wal-Mart's, closed strip-malls, meth labs and people that know for certain that New York and Los Angeles are home to some 'Godamned fruity knickered faggots'.

Bystander. There are plenty of discriminate shootings in America but the indiscriminate shootings are just as commonplace. America has a mass shooting nearly every day. Guns are more than a way of life for Americans they're a way of death. Yes it says something about the gun laws but more than that it says something about the shooters. What the fuck is wrong with young white American men? What's the matter? Got it too fucking good? America needs to talk about Kevin and needs to talk about Kevin pronto. It's getting to the point that if you see an 18-24 year old middle class white kid in an Abercrombie and Fitch t-shirt and a gym bag walking towards you, cross the road.

CIA. Movies tell us that the CIA are a spy agency that works for the government catching bad guys with beards who talk like someone trying to cough a chicken bone out of their throats who smell like incense and prayer matts. Sort of like a bunch of James Bond types with lofty ideals and nifty gadgets who say cool shit like, "Punch in on that number plate". But the reality is that the CIA are a bunch of murderers, drug dealers and arms dealers that operate as a kind of a state sponsored, 'go-getting' sales force for American corporations.

Dream. The American Dream is the one where a great idea and some hard work can turn a kid from nothing into a man with everything. The American Alarm Clock is a bloodless military coup leading to twenty years of illegal wars, serfdom to a corporate oligarchy with the largest wealth disparity of any country in history, a toxic pop culture wasteland filled with celebrity and spectacle in place of substance and 45 million disenfranchised Americans living below the poverty line. And when that alarm clock goes off hitting the snooze button won't be an option.

Emissions. So like Americans like say like every second fucking like word and it's, like, spreading. Thanks to, like, teenagers and, like, shitty pop culture like now the like rest of the world says 'like' every like other like word. It's like (used correctly) America has given the English language word herpes.

Fuckless. America is entering it's 6th decade of a crippling fucks drought which means that America is one of the few countries where fucks are not in plentiful supply. In fact there are large sections of America where there are no fucks at all. Ironically it's this lack of fucks that America has that have helped rise to the super power that it is today. Too many fucks can slow nations down and make it hard to build an Empire. In the past America has been asked by less fortunate for a small 'fuckribution' - but America just kind of shrugs and reminds us all that they are in the middle of a serious fucks shortage and they don't have a single one to give.

Global Reach. The thing about being the dominant super power is that your shit constantly fucks with our shit. You sneeze we get a cold, you explode a nuclear bomb we get a nuclear winter that brings on global extinction event etc. Because of this mighty shit-fucking reach I propose

that we get a say. My proposition is a simple one… we all get 1/10th of a vote in US presidential elections.

Hope Dealer. My fellow Americans. Wanna buy some HOPE? Yo, this shit is the bomb. One hit and you'll be hooked. It's a real mellow high and will placate the shit out of you. It makes you feel like you be doin' *somethin'* about your condition when actually you be doin' *nothin' but doing some hope.*

Infidel? Daddy, What's An Infidel? The real reason the whole terror thing shook America to the core is less about the 'attack' part - that's just the easy part to point to - the anger is just a smoke screen. America is embarrassed. Embarrassed that the they had no fucking clue that a good percentage of the world thought that they're a bunch of spoilt cunts who are responsible for a shit tonne of misery, oppression and a death. Boing! And for 300 million Becky's and Billy's it was the first deviation from the proud parent-like narrative bubble of, "You're an American. You stand for freedom. You're the *good* guys. Everyone loves you." You ever get so embarrassed you kill 1.3 million sand people. It reeks of chubby kids who have been told that they can do anything by their deluded parents and they've turned up to the talent contest only to find out they have no talent. At all. And maybe these wars and invasions are nothing more than a spoilt embarrassed child throwing the mother fucker of all tantrums because they aren't the freedom bringing, freedom flying, GAP model, good guys who can do *anything* they were told they are.

John Wayne. Drink some whiskey, slap a woman, kill an Indian, kiss your gun… get your ass on that stamp you hero.

Kerosine. You don't have to be a 'conspiracy nut' to know that the story we were told about 9/11 is a fucking lie - you just have to be a fan of facts. Here's just one fun fact. Kerosine doesn't burn hot enough to melt steel and that's what jet fuel is - kerosine. So if kerosine can't - never, ever, won't, not, nope, will not, hell-no, it's-impossible-mate, can not - melt steel then don't the American people need to have a serious conversation about the assassination of JFK?

Liberty. Might be time to dismantle that statue and ship that bitch back to France.

Messiah Mania. Rapture Productions Presents. Jesus - American Tour. One Night Only. He will arise! Faithful brought to heaven. Sinners abandoned on Earth. Harps. Angels. Judgements. PLUS pet Dinosaurs on leashes. Coming to your nearest multi million dollar Mega Church. Gayness will be punished. Credit cards will be accepted.

N Word. 'Nigger' is a bad word in the American lexicon because it reminds everyone about a time when white people owned black people. Now white America no longer own black people, instead, they disown them. Progress.

Obese. Not dying of diabetes is now basically a status symbol in America.

Panther. *WE WANT AN IMMEDIATE END TO POLICE BRUTALITY AND MURDER OF BLACK PEOPLE. We believe we can end police brutality in our Black community by organising Black self-defence groups that are dedicated to defending our Black community from racist police oppression and brutality. The second Amendment of the Constitution of the United States gives us the right to bear arms. We therefore believe that all Black people should arm themselves for* *self-defence.* That's point 7 from the Black Panther Party For Self Defence's 10-point program. It was written in 1966 by Black Panther founder Huey P Newton. A revolutionary that today would be called a terrorist. A black organisation that felt cornered by white America and instead of getting scared they got angry, started talking self defence and picked up guns. The Black Panthers would fearlessly police the police in the streets of Oakland. Driving behind patrol cars brandishing fully loaded, entirely legal shotguns ready to draw on law enforcement if they saw the cops 'protecting' the shit out of any black men, women or children. But those were gentler times when a car full of black militants could follow police 'click-clacking' openly loaded guns without recourse. Nowadays Robocop sniper drones point military grade artillery at black mothers holding placards that read DON'T SHOOT I'M UNARMED, while more soldier cops dressed like video game heroes fire tear gas into crowds of black kids with tee-shirts tied around their faces. The scenes playing out on American television look a lot like scenes from Gaza if there was Burger King in Gaza. Imagine what a car filled with armed men dressed in black uniforms, following a patrol car would get! Nuclear fire sent from a bunker in Utah and a cute name like 'Operation Liberty Torch'.

Queen Hillary. As a republic you'd think that America would be anti inherited title and rule. But the Kennedy's, the Bush's and the Clinton's might have something different to say about that.

Retail Therapy. In 2014 Americans spent 51billion dollars shopping… in one day. That day is called Black Friday and you only have to watch video of the Black Friday sales and see a grandmother skull fucking a teenager with remote control over a 90 Inch TV while women and children are trampled by men scrambling to get to a pile of juicers to surmise that the therapist needs a therapist.

Second Amendment. More than the right to bare arms, the second amendment requires a well organised militia to defend the people against its own government in case the government becomes adversarial against it's people… So Obama passed the National Defense Authorization Act making it legal for the military to police it's own citizenry and seize American citizens and hold them without charge. Ahem. Well you NRA trigger monkeys? What the fuck is you waiting for? There's never bee a better time to die for what you believe in. Click-fucking-clack, bros.

Torture. There's a jail in Cuba where America sends it's values and sentences them to death.

"**U**SA! USA! USA!" Americans love to shout the name of their own country which is basically like crying out your own name during sex. This yelling is used to drown out any voice that may like to express ideas that are counter to their own... Ideas like peace, equality or sharing.

Vote. The theory goes that one man has one vote and with that vote they have a say in who represents them in government. The system is called 'Democracy' and on paper its the least terrible of the systems. It was going okay in America until the Cold War with communist Russia when the battle between ideologies got turned into a battle of economies and from that moment democracy was to be forever linked to capitalism. Which is fucked - because the two are opposite belief systems. One is founded on equality and the other is built around gang-fucking the next guy over until the poor cunt is ruined and then doing a hump dance around his burning life and laughing so hard you piss yourself until your Mexican maid has to bring you new khakis. And at this point in the political proceedings there's so much corporate entanglement going on (Hillary raised a staggering $2bn for her run and that wasn't at $20.00 a pop) that every race is essentially the same - two puppets stand up in front of TV cameras and take part in stage produced spectacles filled with concepts dumbed down enough to be written on a hat and play a game of 'put the following words in a sentence'... Folks, freedom, great-again, middle-class, jobs, change, America, way of-life, kids, values, God, and freedom" and then those people who aren't busy watching Wrestle Mania 78 or busy being Black, young or Hispanic go and vote and then 8 years later the candidate who got the most votes gets a book deal and a million bucks a pop to be light entertainment at corporate dinners.

Wall Street. The largest casino on the planet isn't in Vegas it's in Lower Manhattan. It's like a Vegas casino except in this casino it's not pensioners and poor people gambling their life savings it's a bunch of

Ivy league educated, cocaine addicted, high flying, date rapists gambling pensioner's and poor peoples life savings.

Xenophobia. "Build a giant fence because immigrant criminals are coming to take advantage of our education system and health care and are taking our jobs." Said some people that are allergic to books, descended from immigrants and are so fucking shitty at their jobs unwell, uneducated, criminals are taking them.

Yeezus. Celebrities are an American corporate creation designed to pacify and indoctrinate. Like walking, talking advertisements for the worst virtues humanity can muster. They provide a stream of trivia and spectacle that, along with sport, weather and dogs who can skateboard, make up American nightly news. Allowing Americans to Keep Up With The Kardashians even if they aren't keeping up with any other fucking thing. In, like, totally totalitarian double-speak these public relations constructed, script reading, pitch puppets are called 'reality stars' even though their primary role is to distract us from reality. Namely that we have let the planet sour on our watch and no arable lands mean no french fries. Real enough for ya? When you're watching a Kardashian use the lives of their small children as rungs on a ladder or see them lose the battle with addiction (LOL!) or go through a public divorce after the honeymoon period AKA the honeymoon - it's easy to look at reality stars as superficial fun. Until you realise that their secondary role is as educators. Corporate America comes to the rescue as the education system becomes a funnel to jail and Walmart. Reality stars are doing more than just swinging on an athletes dick with eyes like possums. They're teaching us the lessons corporate America so desperately needs us to have our doctorates in. Me Me Me 101, Grandstanding for Beginners, Delusion For Beginners, Self Importance, Manipulation, Comprehensive Greed, Moral Elasticity and Lying For Cruelty And Profit - values that the corporations need us to adopt and hold dear to keep the flickering fuck-fest ticking over. Celebrity and war will be Americas legacy. The Kardashians will be that dying Nations last profitable export and final 'fuck you' to the rest of us… Here's a staggering stat - the average American spends up to 8 hours a day in front of the television - which maybe why they're so fucking average.

Zumba is what the wives of
rich American men do to burn
off all the fat they have on
their body from excess food
consumption. For a shit load
of the women in the rest of
the world they don't have
food access and 'consump-
tion' is a disease of the
lungs.

It's not unfair to say we as a culture are obsessed with beauty. It's a gigantic industry and even bigger con. There couldn't be a more classic piece of bullshit out there that we all unhappily buy into. And at the bottom of that con is this simple fact: beautiful people have a better life than ugly ugly people. Sad to say it but its absolutely true. The more ugly you are the shitter your life will be. If you're rated a 9-10 in the looks department you can expect to live in a parallel universe where handbags boat trips and 345,000 Instagram followers fall from the sky into your lap and your life is free drugs and parties and of course, modelling modeling. A profession where you're only qualifications are... 'being born'. You're the ones in all the ads perpetuating the myth — it's your job to make the rest of us feel shitty about ourselves. Which you're doing so well done, hot stuff. If you're 7-8 out of 10 it's you that are the most caught up in all the celebrity bullshit because you're good looking enough to believe that one day it might be your turn if you just learn the secret or buy the right watch. Good luck. Your best bet is being a background extra/filler/waitress on a super yacht.

You might be able to make money from your looks but you'll probably be wiping cum off some part of your body... bro. 5-6 and you're feeling terrible about yourself pretty much all the time. The advertising out there is pointing out the genetic defect you are. and every time you open a magazine it's like being assaulted by some unseen force. 3-4 you're in politics why can you do something about all this advertising?

After Photo. The world is divided into two camps. The before photos: the lumpy, crooked, chubby, flaky skinned, uglies. And the after photos: The sleek, muscled, shining, Godlike human statues. The after photos are the rulers of nightclubs, workplaces and infomercials everywhere. While the befores... who fucking cares?

$Billions. Your hair is dull and lifeless. Your skin is too dark. Your skin is not dark enough. You have cellulite, stretch marks, wrinkles, suns spots and varicose veins. Your nails are weak, your eyelashes are stunted, the hair on your body makes you look like an animal, your face is all one colour and you smell like a person not a spice rack. You have a gunt, cankles, muffin tops, thunder thighs, bingo wings and belly boobs. Your nose is too long, your chin(s) are too man-ish, you lips are thin and you faces have more lines on them than a mirror at Donatella Versace's house. Now join the other uglies and spend some money, bitch... Because you're worth it.

Collagen. As you age collagen leaves your cells and your skin starts to age. There are many face creams on the market that, promise to increase your collagen to make you look younger but because they cost *hundreds of dollars* they just make you look stupid.

Double D. If you have an ugly nose, crossed-eyes or a face that looks like a punched birthday cake a cosmetic procedure that might work for you is an operation called 'getting some really giant tits'.

Eating Your Feelings. They should really call them Unhappy Meals.

Fatism. Recent polls suggest that fat people are generally considered lazy. It's probably bullshit but the fat, slovenly bastards can't be bothered getting off their lackadaisical arses and setting the record straight.

Guillotine. Women need to lose an average of 23% of their body weight to be considered what they deem as 'perfect'. Maybe leg removal could be the new black?

Hands. With all the cosmetic procedures people are getting it's becoming increasingly hard to decipher the ages of folks. You can make your face look like a balloon stretched over a roast dinner and people won't be able to guess your age – or what species you are -but one glance at those sun beaten wrinkled old claws and everyone will be able to tell that those hands are so old they once held those white iPods that only played music.

Instant Coffee. Have you heard about this new diet where you eat nothing but dry instant coffee with a spoon? You lose 5kgs when all your muscle atrophies because you pass out, fall down some stairs and are in and coma for 3 weeks. #bikinibedsores #nolegmovement #eatthroughanosetube

@Jenseltser is a woman that has an Instagram page with 6million followers. Jen is famous because Jen, apparently, has the most beautiful arse on the planet. Her arse looks like two bald men trying on the same lycra ski-hat at the same time. Like many beautiful people Jen describes what she does as a 'talent'. But her followers probably don't share that opinion – they

only want to put a fork on one butt cheek and knife on the other and eat her arse like a ham.

Kidding Not Kidding. "Let's call it wrinkle prevention serum – cover it pink love hearts and glitter 'n' shit and target 11 year old girls!" – Some marketing guru/vampire somewhere right now.

Liposuction. Maybe if they push the vacuum-needle into you deep enough they'll remove that blackened husk of a soul inside of you as well.

Mirror-Face. Mirror, mirror on the wall who's the 'poutiest, squinting, turning head to one side, taking a big step back, pulling on the crows feet, sighing a big sigh, shaking head and reaching for the make up…' one of all?

News Anchor. How is every person qualified to read the news and do the weather a smoking hot MILF or a do-me-in-your-Cadillac DILF? You'd think that at least one news anchor or weather girl might look, I dunno, weathered?

Orphans. If magazines started saying that chewing the harvested pituitary gland of children could keep one looking young and dewy there'd be a lot of rich white ladies suddenly adopting a lot of poor brown kids…Come to think of it, has anyone seen the chinky eyed Jolie kid lately?

Paralyzed. If you inject enough botulism into the wrinkles on your face the muscles stop working and you lose the ability show any human emotion which is how Nicole Kidman stayed alive all those years under Scientology interrogation.

Q. Why do women wear make upand go on diets?

A. Because they're fat and ugly.

Retouching. Photoshop is an amazing computer program that turns happy teenagers into bulimic head cases.

Selfie. The great news is that when you finally get the black rubbish bag thrust over your head, pushed into a panel van and taken away to a remote warehouse so I can murder you with a hammer for being the worst type of shallow narcissist on the planet - the police will have a ton of those 'super cute' photos you took of yourself to choose from for the missing poster.

Top 10 …ways to combat ankle skin. Top 10 cures for eyebrows. Top 10 ways to stop feet. Top 10 fixes for nose holes. Top 10 finger diets. And 6kgs of perfume ads and you've got yourself a magazine.

Underarm Stubble. Waxing for men is a thing now. Men used to have underarm hair and dignity but it seems you can't have both.

Vagina Lottery. The worst thing about beautiful people is that they act like they had something to do with they look. They act like they are better than the rest of us because of their symmetrical faces and lean bodies - instead of just being eternally grateful they were born lucky… and letting us fondle their boobs / touch their abs.

Wind Tunnel. Plastic surgery makes old women's faces look like a 1997 Toyota Tercel that someone put reading glasses on.

CAP
ITAL
ISM.

Capitalism is probably okay but
we'd never know because that's not
the system we live in. Ours is more
of capitalism for the poor socialism
for the rich type of thing where
the government fucks the poor and
the rich get handouts and support.
I'd say our western system is more
like a Corp-edia-vernment system
where the big three media, government
and corporations have figured out a
delicious the three way orgy of power
and with the use of advertising the
lure of becoming middle management
and the next iPhone kind of got us
right where they want us... and we
in the West are the lucky ones.

Advertising. Like a constant buzzing drone overhead. Advertising reminds us that we are defective and in need of constant upgrades. It's why you feel anxious all the time, get your needs and wants all twisted and why your kids secretly think you're a fucking failure.

Bail Out. Capitalism is ruthless system based on the principles of 'sink or swim'. Your business is either shit and you sink or it's great and you swim. Unless you're a bank then it's more of a 'swim or make a raft out of the bloated corpses of ordinary people's murdered dreams and float off into the sunset' type of thing.

Credit Card Debt. 'Spring Cleaning' is a term we use in the West to describe chucking out all the IKEA, 12 month old electronics, worn-twice shoes and clothes with the wrong logos on them that we bought because we are desperately unhappy and are still paying off at 29% per annum on our credit cards.

Dollar Store. The rich have department stores and the poor have dollar stores. The rich go shopping and come home with a chandelier, a teak table, crystal decanters and some fish eggs that are better travelled than most people. The poor go shopping and come home with some electric candles a TV dinner tray a crystal meth decanter and a plastic fish that sings, "Holiday." By Madonna.

Environment. If your house was burning down what would you save? It's one of those pseudo revealing questions people ask celebrities in interviews that are printed in the backs of Sunday magazines - or speed dating applicants ask each other before going home to their cats and avatars. It gives the actor /model an opportunity to answer the question in such a way that makes themselves look sensitive but also do a public inventory of the stuff they own. It's a hypothetical question designed to be illustrative because if your house is really on fire the real question is, which karate kick do you use on which family member to knock them down so you can you clamber over them, the acoustic guitar your father wooed your mother on, the photos of your twin brother who died when you were both 16 and the ballet shoes your great grandmother smuggled through Auschwitz (that made her remember how freedom felt) to get to your laptop and phone and rush them out of the house before the flames melt your memoirs and passwords. It's a question of priorities. But your house isn't burning down - probably. You, your laptop and your dusty tat are safe and sound. However the world on which your house stands is not in great shape. The Earth is well and truly on fire. Every serious scientist in the world that doesn't have oil under his fingernails is now saying that we've, "Fucked this planet up right nice…" (their words - not mine) and it seems we've reached the point of no return where fixing what we've done to Mother Earth might not be an option - we really are bunch of Mother fuckers. You know those movies where someone's parents leave for the weekend and before they leave they say, "Tyler. Look at me. NO PARTIES." Well, we are Tyler and we've woken up with a pool toy round our midriffs and bong the shape of a penis in our hands and we *totally can't believe* what happened to our parents house. If the world was a house:

The living room would be a bombed out wreckage with a tiny child holding a dolls head in her hand asking no one in particular why the drone killed her Daddy and what genocide is? The kitchen would be too radioactive to go into and besides you don't want to wake up the giant nuclear mutant Japanese Lizard that eats cars and destroys cities. The spare room would be filled with water but not the drinkable kind, the angry kind that… floods spare rooms. The bedroom would be jammed full of sick people all coughing an d dying from some medicine resistant epidemic caused by Jenny McCarthy and the vaccine deniers. The hallway would be one bony polar bear with yellow fur sitting on a stack of unused phonebooks asking to bum a fag. The Attic would be some middleclass English folks putting their bottles and cans in the correct recycling bins and making compost for their allotments with their fingers crossed so hard they make creaking sounds when they shake hands. And the garage would be filled with Americans taking photos of themselves on the bonnets of their 4WD's saying "LALALALALA" with their fingers in their ears deciding where to go to brunch. At worst we are looking at what they call an 'Extinction Event' where the human race ends exploding in a rain of plastic confetti and the Earth is left for what ever land creatures and sea creatures remain who can then battle it out for global supremacy finally answering the question every stoned teenager has asked

- "who would win in fight between a Shark and Tiger?" At best a few billion people will die including some of the climate change deniers which would be a sweet 'I told you so' moment if we weren't fighting for our lives pretty much constantly and all suicidal because our socks are always damp. We could - crazy idea - make dramatic changes to the way we live on this planet but it would mean everyone - I mean everyone - would have to all do it at once. Stop using oil to melt steel, stop charging their iPhone, stop eating asparagus from Spain and probably not have a holiday this year. BUT even if we could agree to give it rest some prick will melt a bit of steel and build something cool like a shopping mall with a rollercoaster in it while the rest of us are darning our trousers with pubic hair and cactus needles and then we'll all be like, "Hey look China is still melting steel and eating Spanish asparagus. Fuck this!" And then before you can say, "My iPhone's fully charged" we'll all be eating 'esparragos' on our new rollercoaster - pinkys out! So bottom line: We're fucked. Stop wasting all of your time. If you do something you hate. Stop doing that thing.

If someone's a dick to you. Tell that someone to fuck off. Get high and jump into the sea. It's fuckin' over. You're free.

FIAT Currency. Toilet paper is made by taking wood and soaking it in chemicals and creating pulp. This pulp is then laid out and dried and pressed... then the print some dead presidents or pictures of the queen on it and voila - perfect to wipe your arse on.

Greed. Here's an ethics question: Imagine there's a button that you can push and when you do you get a million dollars BUT someone you don't know, a total stranger, drops dead... Question - What's the best way of treating repetitive strain injury in ones button-pushing finger?

Hundredaires. These days the world is broken up into four demographics.
Hundredaires - Money is food and fuel.
Thousandaires. Money is debt.
Millionaires. Money is time.
Billionaires. Money is power.
If you're a Thousandaire, congrats. The fact that you have a house (you bought with a 90% mortgage and are one missed payment away from handing to the bank and moving in to your parent's... station wagon) and

the fact that your kids (probably named Taylor and Jordan because you think they sound like rich names) have some food in their bellies and wear 'outfits' to school (made by nimble little fingers of other children) means that you are considered by the UN as 'rich' and compared to billions of other human beings on the planet, wringing out drinking water from camel dung and eating grass soup for dinner, you are - but we both know you aren't. You're the guy in the Hyundai, happy because you got the 9th stamp on your Starbucks card and your favourite sporting team is playing that night. You're on the way to do a deal whereby a new building development buys 120 air-conditioning units from the company you work for and you stand to make an extra 458.98 in bonuses this month… And then a $200,000 super car blows by you on the freeway and you, the air-con guy with the full loyalty card, feels shitty about himself and slightly sorry for your wife. That's us. We're not rich-rich. Not magic rich. Rich to the point you no longer carry money. So rich you point at things and the things rise and float to your grasp or are killed or they lay back on a bed and slip the point of a 6 inch high heel up their rectum while you stroke a lazy erection. So rich that you become a deity and see the rest of us as chimpanzees and can only empathize with us as pets or resources (at best). Where the people around you are either totally silent or supremely scintillating - no one talks to you about the weather or their stupid feelings. You never hear about anything that doesn't directly interest you or benefit you. Where you can have and do whatever you want to whomever you see whenever you like. That rich. And there are people out there like that. It's 'them' and 'us'. Them (the 1%) own the things that we (the 99%) think are ours. They own our opinions and our facts. They own our homes. They own our information. They own our time. They own our health. The 99% are angry at the 1% for having 99% of all the money and 100% of the 1% give 0% of a fuck. We hate the rich and the rich couldn't care less. Usually when the 1% care this little about something, raising their kids for example, they pay someone poor to do that caring for them but in this case they haven't even bothered to do that. They couldn't muster a fuck to give. They don't care that you held up little placards covered with scrawls of crayon and sat on the steps of their temples or blogged about it on 'your' Internet. They don't care that we blame them for 'this mess we're in' they are too busy being nasty little murder-addicted-rape-apes, eating endangered species, divorcing women as a sport and wearing red chinos. Red chinos! The horror! Besides they probably can't hear us over their chopper blades – and who do you think you bought the crayons and placard paper from in the first place?

Income Tax. When you are born into a capitalist society you become a sort of slave that works until Wednesday lunch time for nothing – this is because 97% of the money in circulation exists based on debt and it's you that's paying it off. Now have some coffee and get back in there, champ. Your production is waning.

Jobless. Not having a job in a capitalist society is akin to having Harry Potter's cloak of invisibility stapled to your body except a cloak might actually keep you dry and warm when the wind sweeps the rain into the doorway and soaks your cardboard bed through.

Kidney. One careful owner One job that's always available to poor people is Organ Farmer. What it involves is having some organs inside your body for a really long time – probably until you're an adult and then cutting a couple out of yourself and selling them to a rich person. You don't get rich but you don't stay poor either – because you die.

Loop Hole. Google, Amazon, Wal-Mart all the big corporations pay no tax. Instead they pay lawyers to find loopholes that get them out of paying tax. If you or me didn't pay tax you'd have to pay a lawyer too – but their job would be to try and get you out of jail.

Mr. Baker. When you work in a capitalist system an imaginary hierarchy exists where one man is better than another man based on how much money they have. If anyone has ever said to you, "You don't have to call me Mr. Baker – just call me Bob." What that means is "I am Bob and I is your Daddy."

Ninety-nine. We are a bunch of morons. I'm surprised the whole human race is not stuck at the bottom of a well. You know why? Because we collectively believe something that costs $999.99 is cheaper than something that costs $1000.00.

Oligarch. When communism collapsed in Russia the government gave away all the country`s resources to a few ex KGB thugs. Even though they aren't officially criminals they have been on a crime spree against denim and good music ever since they got rich.

Pay Day. If you know what day is payday - you're probably poor.

Quantitative Easing. The best thing about the fact that there are actual metric tons of cash floating around is that when it all topples over and the riots start - you can duct tape bundles of it to yourself as a rudimentary stab-proofing, stuff it into your clothes for extra warmth or burn it to start a fire to smoke your enemies out of the network of underground sewers they are hiding in so you can enslave their women and eat their children.

Reflexology. The world is rapidly dividing into two camps - those with money and the rest of us that go to war and die, fetch things, dance in underwear and massage the reptilian skin on the pampered feet of those with money.

Slavery. It got so bad at the Apple factory that they had to put up suicide nets to stop the slaves from ending their own lives. However Apple would prefer it if you didn't called them 'suicide nets' - they prefer the term 'spontaneous rest hammocks'.

Trickle Up Theory. So the story goes that the government gives tax breaks and bailouts to the richest people in the world and then the rich people create jobs for the rest of us and the money 'trickles down' to us. You know what else trickles downwards? Bull shit.

Uniformity. Have you noticed that everywhere you go is exactly the same? Everywhere you look - identical: The Gap next to a Starbucks across from the same McDonalds beside the same Body Shop near the same homeless person drinking the same methylated spirits pissing on himself with the same expression of hopelessness etched onto his face...

Victoria's Secret Model. Women who wear undies for a living are another perk for guys who are winning at capitalism. These female sex giraffes don't fuck guys named Ned who own Kia 4X4's they only fuck guys named Serge who own Ned.

White Men. If you're not a soft bellied white man it's very unlikely that you're getting the full benefit of capitalism. Capitalism is a system developed by putty dicked white men to make up for their inability to run, throw, fight or survive in the wild faced with anything more than a drizzle. So instead of constantly getting their arses handed to them they invented being the 'boss' and now running throwing fighting or surviving is only done on the TV networks they own.

X12275CT55567. Will be your name in the future when you are a micro chipped citizen. It will be easy to remember because it will be tattooed on your forehead " *Enjoy your ground insect based protein paste and report for delousing before entering the plasma-fuel donation center where you'll be donating your blood to keep the robot soldiers that killed your wife for queue jumping running on plasma fuels cells, X12275CT55567 you organic being.*"

Yorkshire Terrier. After the revolution comes and the mansions are stormed, sacked and looted. After the people rise up and climb over the iron gates and murder the inhabitants of the gin palaces with guns they have wrenched from the hands of dead cops. After the tables have finally turned - the tiny, embarrassed lap dogs will come out of hiding from their $20,000.00 hand bags prisons to eat the faces off their decomposing owners and know what it is to be wolves once more!

Zucchini Chips. The Middle Class think they're doing well but their kids go to school in a broken system, their houses are owned by the banks, they work in jobs they hate and Zucchini chips taste like fucking nothing.

Scramble, deal, pray, fight, kick, cryogenically freeze yourself or download your consciousness onto a ~~comptur~~ computer — you'll still die. Your only hope is to die well. Without embarrassing false surety of the after life religion promises, the bullshit reason to die patriotism gives us or full of regret, bitterness and anger that being entombed in your own self deceit will surely bring. To die surrounded by some people that actually love you means you've lived your life to some sort of code and been, at least for the most part, honest. But spending any length of time on this rock surrounded by the worst humanity has to offer will practically guarantee a death filled with remorse anger and the smell of cancer. Good luck flesh-made fuck-wit. Good luck and enjoy the inky sweet release of the blackness.

AIDS. I had such great hopes for you, AIDS. Especially when you made the jump from homos and junkies to us regular folks. I thought, "This is great I'll always get a seat on the train now." But then you pussied out and got all manageable 'n' shit like some sort of back injury or skin condition. A piddly 39 million people dead since you started doing your thing. 150 Americans die everyday in work related injuries! Jesus Christ AIDS, you're now not even as deadly as a damp scaffolding plank.

Blasphemy. A good rule of thumb is not to talk shit about crazy people's imaginary friends especially if their imaginary friends wrote a book about love and forgiveness.

Cancer. Okay so-called 'greatest minds in a generation' you had a crack at curing cancer and you failed. Everyone white basically dies from it (if you're brown or black your fate is generally more dramatic and often way more bullety). Now let's just admit that we got beat by it and get the focus back on to the hover boards, jet packs and teleportation please.

Darwinism. Some people are allergic to nuts. Even touching a peanut could kill them. Letting these weaklings live is counter to the survival of the human race. My call is to round them all up, lock them in a warehouse for two weeks and slide some snickers bars under the door.

Ebola. When Mother Nature does her spring-cleaning she doesn't use a broom. She uses a nifty little virus that makes you shit your organs, fills your eyes with blood and spreads faster than a cat on the Internet asking for a cheezburger. Maybe it's their cute little faces, their grasping little hands or their agile prehensile tails? Whatever it is there's no denying that African monkey pussy seems to be pretty damn irresistible and every time we fuck it we seem to be going in bareback.

FOMO. Can people really 'look down' from Heaven? Or is it like they've graduated from Earth and this mortal coil and they're too cool now. "Oh yeah - sorry I didn't get back to you - you know… I've been all busy with things." And when you go to Heaven and join them it's fucking awkward because they've been ignoring you and not doing as much 'looking down' as they should and you're all, "What about that thing with the gas tank?" and they have to act like they know about it like, "Oh that! That was crazy, right?" and you both know it's bullshit, and then God says "Awkwaaaard!" and fist bumps with St. Peter and they both disappear to play petanque and drink wine out of jam jars.

Germs. When you're a kid they explain everything to you by drawing a face on the thing they want you to know about and either making it an angry face or a happy face. So if they want you to eat your vegetables they draw a Zucchini with a face on it that looks like it's being sucked off on a waterbed by a trucker's wife or a red cabbage that looks like it's swallowed an ecstasy factory. But when they want to tell you something is bad they draw an angry face on it that looks like a despotic overlord who rules his minions with a series of growling threats and by blinking fast. So when people talk about super-bugs that are immune to our antibiotics I think of some sad face little white pills being gang raped by a whole lot of ISIS faced germs while a Stalin faced overlord looks on feasting on a crying antibody wearing a wig and lipstick.

Homicide. Murder is about to become a growth industry. The longer you spend on this planet the more you realise that life is just a series of situations where you desperately try not to murder some prick. Everyday more eligible pricks seem to be turning up to every situation kind of begging you to murder the shit out of them. It's a matter of time before the floodgates open and murder is de rigour. I believe we'll need to do a couple of things. One - build incinerators. Two - evaluate the punitive nature of our justice system. It's time for a pivot. So instead of being punished for murdering we should actually be rewarded for not murdering. Like frequent flyer miles, we should be given tokens at the end of every year that we don't murder (double points if you use public transport). "Well done! For not murdering, sir. Here's your 1 year murder-free token." Then you can take your tokens into your local megamart and cash them in for a panini grill.

Immortality. If given the gift of immortality and an eternity of life we like to think we would master all the languages, travel the seas and oceans, taste every fruit and animal on the planet, read every great book written and become the fulfillment of our vast human potential. But we all know that's patently untrue. We'd probably... just kind of hang around and procrastinate until we were the last person on earth and then get all pissy because no ones making any more electricity and we need to charge our iPhone 223 if we're ever going to get off level 56 of Candy Crush.

Joseph Stalin said: one man's death is a tragedy, 10,000 is a statistic. I reckon he was half right.

Klingon. It's this point in our relationship with this planet I think it's time we tripled our efforts to contact alien life and when we have found them ask them if they could... go and fuck themselves and then call them a bunch of cunts. We need a warlike alien species to destroy us and all the evidence of one of the greatest fuck ups in galactic history.

Lungs. Ever see a smoker puffing a Marlborough through their tracheotomy? It makes seeing a crack-head letting a truck driver slap her round and piss on her in a vacant lot behind a gas station for a $10.00 rock look tame and reasonable.

Memory. Aww shit what's that brain thing that's killing me slowly? It comes from all those late nights, stress and alcohol... You know? Fuck? Oh jeeez... It's called. Wait hold on.... Umm. It's on the tip of my tongue.

National Anthem. Patriotism is a terrible and deadly disease. Generally contracted after some imagined slight against the hosts 'nation'. Patriotism can cause the host to group with other infected people and go and get their arms and legs and heads blown up by IED's in some shit hole of a desert. Which is the only known cure.

0800 HELPLINE. Suicide is considered an extremely selfish act and I agree. You could be helping society. If you are going to kill yourself you should at least have the decency to donate yourself to a pervert so they can get some of that weird sex stuff out of their system. What's the differ-ence if you get your pubes burnt off with some birth-day candles and your mouth treated like a potty before you kick the chair out from under you?

Plutonium. There are about 17,300 nuclear warheads in the world and it's estimat-ed that it would only take 100 warheads to bring about a Nuclear winter that would end humanity. All except the uber-nerds in the un-derground bunkers who will emerge in 100 years rubbing their eyes and repopulate the world with the weakest most bullyable offspring the universe has ever known.

Quentin Tarantino. In my experience of violence no one is saying cool-guy dialogue. I once watched a fight where one guy was getting beaten up and he was screaming out "I've shit in my pants. I've shit in my pants." Had he died those would have been his last words.

Real Thing. I'd like to teach the world to sing, in perfect harmony. I'd like to buy the world a coke… but I'm a 13 year old with an amputated foot in a diabetic coma.

Serial Killer. There are plenty of murderers and lots of mass murderers but the killers that capture our imaginations are the serial killers. So if you're sit-ting in your room detailing your coming spree in really, really, small hand writ-ing or you've made that big step and and started murder-ing school girls and leav-ing playing cards wedged in their vaginas don't pussy out and stop at four. You need to murder at least five girls to be considered a serial killer. If you don't kill at least five you're not a serial killer you're just a murderer with a very, very elaborate card trick.

Texting. JST CRSHING HED FRST IN2 A SCHL BUS. BRB

Uner Tan Syndrome. The great thing about diagnos-ing your own health prob-lems online is you get to the bottom of your rare and incurable disease without 'medical' advice from peo-ple who won't stop chucking their know-all diplomas in your face! Now I'm off to fill a bath with newt blood - I have to cure my echoing brain syndrome.

Vaccine. I'm working on a vaccine that vaccinates against the stupidity of anti-vaccinators. It's a baseball bat with three nails in it and it's definitely intramuscular.

Widower. If you're making love to your wife and she dies in your arms. What would you do? Would you... keep going until you cum? I have decided that I would... But only if I was 3... no 5 stokes away. I think 5 strokes is fine. Anything more than 5 and it's necrophilia - but I think 5 is completely justifiable. Okay 5 strokes and one postion change. Okay 5 strokes, one position change and bit of arse play - then I'll call the ambulance.

X-Ray. If you want to see inside someone you need an x-ray machine. You just show them an x-ray of that shadow on their lung and they'll vomit their insides into the waste paper bin in your office.

Yosemite. Anyone climbing mountains without ropes is a fuck-wit and the only people who should shed a tear when they eventually splash onto rocks should be the makers of dreadlock wax and hacky sacks.

Zealot. There are some people that claim to be unafraid of death. They are Religious people. According to them - the good bit of life is death. They have nothing to live for and everything to die for. The great news is that this belief finally allows some common ground between us normal people and the religious fuck-nuts. We're both looking forward to their eventual demise.

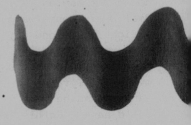

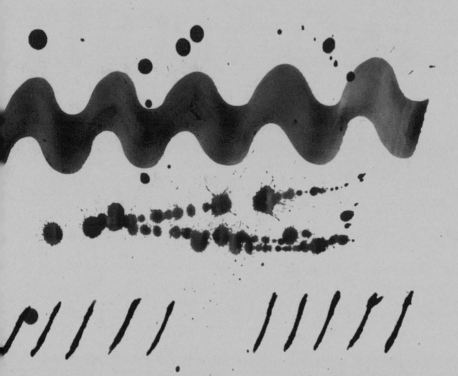

Going to work is like dying in slow motion.
It gives ~~people~~ good people cancer and
bad people power. It's an affront to who
we are as animals. Offices are a breeding
ground for power hungry little peon cunts who,
if all things were equal ~~and we were we~~
~~were happiest~~, wouldn't have made it out
of adolescence without being pushed in front
of a lion. It rewards the most crawling
and despicable mediocrity and has given
rise to a new lexicon which no one from
a time when work was noble would even
fucking recognise. Burn the offices,
lynch the managers and throw
the water coolers into the sea.

Acronyms. B.T.W. - When I had a job I spoke in acronyms, as I was too busy to say whole sentences. And FYI, I even used U.A.'s - AKA 'unnecessary acronyms'. And in a moment of meta genius I started pronouncing the acronyms as actual words to save valuable zilli-seconds beeteedoubleuew, eff-whyeye.

Brainstorm. Is there a more hateful phrase in our lexicon? I'd rather be invited to a prison rape than to another Brainstorm. I'd rather be led by the hand into a quiet corner of Tier 5 by some 3-strike-lifers with shanks than to be ushered into the 'Opus room' for an 'opportunity' to 'add value' to a clients business with a '360 holistic approach to the media landscape' led by some sebaceous middle management bot holding on to the white board marker like Gollum holding the One Ring.

Cubicles. When chickens are kept in battery cages they go insane and peck each other to death - this is because they aren't allowed to personalize their space with 4-7 family photos and a poster of a cat - if they could they'd only die inside and go limp on a swivel chair until their hearts fail like we do.

Deskatarian. Every piece of food that goes into the work microwave ends up making the whole office smell like farts.

Elevator Chat. There's a specific brand of meaningless conversation that happens in elevators between floors in your office. Worse than straight up weather talk or the back'n'forths dog owners enjoy, this chat actually injures the human soul to the point of near death. That's why it's best to just stare at the numbers and concentrate on the slow release of air out of your sphincter without making the fart noise.

Friends. Work friends are not your friends. If someone likes you at work they don't like the real you they like work you. Work you is a nice person who likes sandwiches and 'had a good weekend'. Real you is a borderline racist who buys prostitutes toenail clippings online and cries in the shower until the water runs cold.

Grovelling. What's that noise? Is that your voice? What the fuck happened to your voice? When did it become that super polite nice sounding thing? You sound like a kindergarten teacher try into explain the holocaust to a room full of 6-year-olds. Holy fuck what was that? Was that a laugh? Why? Why did you laugh? Nothing that fat cunt said was funny. Stop that laughing. Oh my God. Don't ask him about his kids… why did you do that? Now he's telling you about his fucking kids. What the fuck is wrong with you? Oh my God- what is that voice! What the fuck - who are you? I don't even know who you are anymore.

HR. Everyone is all super sensitive to sexual harassment in the workplace now. You can't even make a polite comment about the shape of a colleagues tits or ask if your homosexual work mate sucked any nice dicks on the weekend without someone dropping a dime on you to human resources. It's political correctness gone mad. It used to be that it wasn't considered harassment unless you refused to pay your half for the abortion.

I in Team. It's true that there is no I in team. But if you look I think you'll find there is a U in CUNT.

Jaipur. Thanks for all your hard work but we've decided to out source your job to India where we can pay people shit and they don't constantly knock on our door asking about 'their future'

and believing they're meant for better things. That nonsense is fucking exhausting. -Management

Kidless. Sadness has a new mascot - it's a 44 year old woman sitting at her desk punching numbers into an excel spreadsheet in a windowless office being told that because she waited so long to have kids her womb is now full of asbestos and broken pipes and is basically an uninhabitable bunker littered with egg shells, sperm carcasses and Robert Duval howling like shot sea lion.

LOTTO. Here's a question Mrs. "I love my work"… Here's a query Mr. "Do what you love and you'll never work a day in your life…" Say you win Lotto this Saturday and you suddenly have 213 million dollars in the bank - are you strapping on you stupid 'team work' face and heading into the ol' office for some blue sky thinking and some project planning or are you heading to where the sky is blue and start planning project 'do what ever the fuck I want forever'?

Middle Management. The greatest trick the boss classes ever pulled on us is Middle Management. You now have all the responsibility and none of the power - sound good? All you need to do is snitch on your brothers and sisters, keep track of their whereabouts and make sure Glenn isn't wasting post-it-notes. And if you do that - we'll give you a different coloured uniform. For that uniform you'll be in on the weekend, work until 9pm, eat lunch at your desk, have to have a relationship with a workmate and watch summer after summer pass by your window while the rest of us look at you with pity in our hearts… or is that envy?

Nice. Rule 28. If you can't great be nice. So be nice, Janice you know-it-all whore.

Out Of Office. Dear anyone who needs me to do that soul crushing thing. You may go and fuck yourself. Not gently. But with the fury of a 100 storms. I am not worker me any longer I am holiday me and I have some hats that I have been wondering if I can get away with. If you need anything contact Janice who is a poor facsimile of me and will do nothing to help you so that when i return after 2 weeks there will be a raging fire in my inbox and I will want to kill myself. BUT THAT WILL BE THEN AND NOW IT IS NOW. AND NOW IS MORE GLORIOUS THAN NEW LIFE.

Power Point. It's neither powerful or makes a point. It is for the powerless who have no point. It should be called ShitLister, HereComeTheLies, or PleasePlease-GiveUsMoney. I sometimes imagine the meeting where the software designers presented PowerPoint but this was before PowerPoint. How did they manage to sell it? I imagine they all just took a shit in a bucket and mixed the shit up with a bit of urine got nude and spread it all over the walls like a dirty protest. Mashing handfuls of feces on glass bricks and powder blue paint and then said - "Ladies and Gentlemen, I give you Power-Point. This will ruin every-thing."

Quit. You are not your job! You are more than that salary! Quit your job. Free yourself from the tyranny of the 9 to 5 and then six months later free yourself from the tyranny of having a roof over your head.

Remuneration. If you have a very terrible fucking shitty job you'll get paid every day. If your job is just fucked and painful you'll be getting an envelope once a week. If you get paid once a month you have a decent job and if you get paid once a year - fuck you we all hope you get a fast acting cancer and can take none of it with you.

Sandra. "Just playing devils advocate but...what about... the opposite of what you just said forever and always? Because I'm Sandra and that's what I do. Just throw spanners at things? How about that?" Good point Sandra but how about, "Fuck you, you childless wreck of a cunt! FUCK YOU you barnacle on the boat of progress. FUCK you and every other Sandra like you! This fucking job is shitty enough without you making it worse by existing. I'm going to actively hate you now for the rest of the day. What's the job number for HATING A BITCH, Sandra? Or shall I just put it under INTERNAL?

Tea. Because procrastination is thirsty work.

Unimportant. The problem we have as a bunch of Western World work monkeys is that our work is so unimportant. It's just meetings about meetings. No company has any more money to actually make anything come out of the end of this binary driven sausage machine. They only have enough money to keep the sick machine working. We all get paid to work but no one is getting paid to finish - the work is the outcome no longer the process. It's just a trap to keep us from organising as a collective of revolutionaries and collectively organising the building of ace water parks and drinking beer with our mates.

Vanity Smurf. Now, there are two types of Smurfs. The Smurfs who are named after their personality IE: Vanity Smurf and Jokey Smurf - the happy ones. And the other type who are named what their job is IE: Handy Smurf and Painter Smurf - the ones who have no hope of ever smurfing Smurfette in the Smurf. The point is: Some Smurfs are what they do and some Smurfs do who they are. And that's the reason everything isn't Smurfy for most of us Smurfs. Most of us aren't Model/Actor Smurf, we're Fiscal Report Smurf. We're Food Prep Smurf... We're Brainstorm Smurf.

Weekend. Monday = depression. Tuesday = resignation. Wednesday = numbness. Thursday = hope. Friday = excitement. Saturday = joy. Sunday = dread. Repeat until death.

Xeroxed Buttholes. At the end of the year most offices throw a party giving people a plethora of really interesting ways to resign.

YOLO. You will spend 4166 days at work in your lifetime. These days will never be retrieved and none of them will feature in any fond memories you have on your deathbed. Instead, they will be the beige regrets that will give you one last burst of anger about the way you punted your whole life as the last breath slips from your translucent frame.

Zastava M85. The Zastava M85 is a rifle designed and produced by Yugoslavian killing machine maker Zastava Arms. The M85 is practically the same as the carbine version of the M70 and Zastava M92, the only difference being in caliber, and in this case, the magazine design. It would easily fit into a gym bag and make Monday morning's status meeting end. Forever.

FASHION

Fashion is sport for homos.
That's what all you fashion haters
(fat chicks and straight men) need
to remember. But unlike sports
fashion creates and funds art and
art is good. There are down sides of
course like dead brown kids crushed
under unsafe tee-shirt factories
and jeggings but without it we'd
have a whole lot of bored homosexual
men and way flamboyant middle-aged
women ~~squaking~~ squawking at the TV,
giving a shit about 'the game' and
yelling out "KISS! KISS! KISS! Every
time someone's tackled.

Anorexia Nervosa. Not eating is and always will, be tres chic. If you need to get nutrients get them from cigarette smoke and if you must have a meal eat with your nostrils. As Kate Moss says, 'Nothing tastes as good as skinny feels."

Black. Trend Alert. Black is the new black. The old black was also black and the next black will probably be black too.

Cat Walk. If you have 2 minutes watching models try to stay 'fierce' while they fall over in high heels in front of po-faced fashionistas is up there with fat people try to water ski.

Do's and Don'ts. There really aren't any anymore. As Muccia Prada says, "Everything is in fashion all at once all the time." So don't sweat it you Sport Goth Haute Rave Chanel bunny.

Envy. A multi billion dollar industry built around the simple fact that she looks waaayyy better than you do.

Fashion TV. The fashion channel. It's this season's collection highlights and model profiles 24/7. Basically it's ESPN for homosexuals.

Gays. You know why you can't wear anything you see on the catwalk? Gay men run fashion and gay men are allergic to tits.

Handbags. An authentic Hermes Birkin bag costs around $20k or you can buy a replica for around $200. This means no matter how good the replica is they're easy to spot… if someone like you has one - it's a replica.

Instagram. Instagram is the home of the off-duty model so if you're momentarily feeling good about yourself - log on, check out their lives and get back to feeling wretched.

J Lo. Every now and then some goofy Popstar will try and do a fashion line and it always fails. J Lo, for example, lost money on a line that looked like someone threw a diamanté grenade into an Eastern European denim factory.

Kilts. Inevitably some designer will throw some silly shit like kilts down the runway and keep a straight face. Last year they wanted us wearing capes next year we'll be expected to go to work wearing a fish bowl on our genitals.

Logo. This is how it works: Tee shirt without logo = $10.00. Tee shirt with logo = $100.00. So they're not just tee shirts - they're IQ tests.

Modelling Agency. Agencies are the pimps of the fashion world. There's an outcry at the moment because models are claiming they're mistreated. Really? You work long hours, and you get pressure to be skinny - and then what happens? You get paid a normal person's week's wages in an hour for wearing some pants and looking bored.
You call it mistreatment - we call it cunt tax.

NYFW. New York Fashion Week is where you go if you're a designer who wants to shop a collection, you're a model who wants to get discovered or you're an Oligarch who wants to finger a model.

OMG. "OMG! OMG! OMG! OMG! *(breath)* OMG! OMG! OMG! OMG! OMG!"

Photographer. Everyone's got a style blog and everyone's a photographer… except photographers - they're now 'collaborators' (loads gun holds it to own head).

Quirky. 'Quirky' is the look you need to go for if you are, what they call in fashion, 'Ugly'.

Rhianna. Rhi Rhi gets paid $100k to sit in the front row of shows and get designers some attention. Which makes her an overpriced accessory used to sell over priced accessories.

Super Models. These are people's 'favourite models'. If fashion is art then models are the blank walls that the art hangs on. Having a favorite model is like having a favorite shade of white paint.

Terry Richardson. Uncle Terry is a fashion mainstay and also a rapey old fuck who likes to take photos of models touching his giant cock. The models complain but being photographed next to that fat veiny piece is a great way to look skinny.

Urban. What the fashion industry calls black people. As in, "Let's price it high enough so that those urbans can't afford it."

Vogue. Vogue is considered the fashion bible. It's edited by Anna Wintour; a woman who came out of an egg and sleeps inside the cadavers of failed teenage models. I bet her breath smells like every poo she hasn't had since 2002.

Wearable Fashion. Code for what people actually wear. So say a woman walks down the runway wearing a very couture ensemble made from dinghy oars with a seagull on her head - how that translates to the real-world is jeans and a tee-shirt. Wearable.

X x x. "Mwah! Mwah! Mwah! You look too fabulous. Dahhling we must hook up." Yes people in fashion actually talk like that. Tools.

Youth. Attention mutton dressed as lamb. You know who you are. Stop it.

Zoolander. A hard-hitting documentary that lifted the lid on the vacuous nature of the fashion world. A must see for any aspiring fashionista.

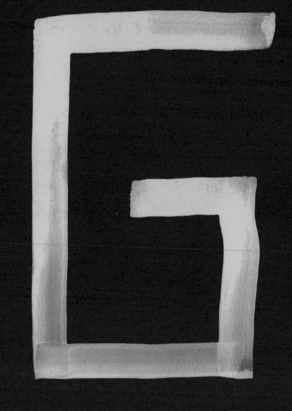

GASTRONOMY

All food turns to shit and should be treated that way. The fetishizing of food is a bi-product of our bloated excess and history shows us that every time food is worshipped like it is now it's near the end of that particular civilization. Rome had celebrity chefs and then they had wide spread starvation and murdering. We're all eating Denial Pie in a 'gastro pub slash café slash communal dining concept'! Plus nothing you can do in your fancy arsed eatery tastes better than fresh meat cooked on a hot fire or a fish in a leaf in some coals. And nothing is better to drink than cold coconut water. Is there anything worse than insuffrable cunt asking a whole lot of questions about the food to a waiter? It makes you look like the soft bellied leech you are and will get your locally sourced, macro biotic, shrub based, fallen not picked, Lithanium mash-up food spat in.

Asparagus Piss. If your defecation is known a 'Number 2' and your urination is known as a 'Number 1' – then an asparagus piss is a 'number 1.5' and you're not a human being if you don't secretly close your eyes and smell that weird, wonderful odor and smile out the side of your face.

Bacon. Some people say human beings are supposed to be vegetarian. If anyone ever needed an argument against that croc of shit the best argument is the smell of bacon cooking. That shit is primal. Get the right amount of bacon cooking on the right morning and watch Minerva and Farquah stop doing yoga, spit out their sprouts, shave off their dreadlocks and push some children over trying to get that pork on their hand carved fork.

Chicken. We eat more chicken than any other animal. It's easily the most popular animal. If chicken knew how everything copied the way it tasted – chickens would be walking around with a real swagger in their step and would be insufferable to be with at parties.

Dinner Party. Sometimes food isn't actually for providing nutrition sometimes. It's for making your friends feel like failures. It's for turning your friends from decent people to a bunch of tasteless heathens who should bow down and kiss the hem of your apron because you can stuff a capsicum with gorgonzola and know what setting your oven needs to be at to keep your quail moist and they brought a $9.00 bottle of wine with them (in a supermarket bag). Common cunts.

Eggs. Never put chicken into an egg omelet - you'll just sit there staring at it wondering which bit to eat first.

Fois Gras. Being at the top of the food chain not something we as humans take lightly. We could just do what we do and eat EVERYTHING with a face that bares young and be happy with that. But nope - not enough. To really assert our dominance we make sure we are as cruel as we can be to the animal before we kill it and eat it. Why? Because fuck you goose! That's why.

Gravy Sweat. When fat people sweat it's a thick viscous fluid that can be scraped out of their waxen folds and used as bearing grease, fire starter or to bait traps to catch wild dogs.

Heart Burn. When you eat a meal and you're full but you keep stuffing food into your face… just stuffing and jamming food into your mouth hole to stop the pain of loneliness and the emptiness of your failed life experiment sometimes stomach acid tries to rise up and climb up into your torso to stop the influx of half-chewed matter like stomach tears from the cries for help from inside you. That's heartburn and you'll need to swallow some medicine if you want to dull the pain and continue your pastry covered suicide mission.

Instagram. It used to be that before we ate something we'd shoot it. Now before we eat something we shoot it.

Juicer. Next we'll just be taking our food and throwing it straight into the toilet.

Kale. If pressed, no one *actually* knows what Kale is - not even the places that serve it. 9 times out of 10 they serve dried spinach and the other one time it's just the steam that comes off your meal.

Lasagna. Your mother used to cook that amazing lasagna that tasted of love and care. It would fill you with a feeling of safety and make your heart smile. But now you eat cereal in front of the TV because Mommy's cleans an office until 2am since Daddy left you guys in the middle of the night.

Michelin Star. At this level food becomes art and people twat on about experience this and refined that - but when all is said and done and the thistle flower foam and dessert that looks like a pile of earth is cleared away - what you're left with is a $300.00 poo.

Neohesperidin Dihydrochalcone. Say your sister owes you money but the crack head bitch won't pay you back. Offer to baby-sit her kids for the afternoon. Do some kid-crap with them for a couple of hours but then right before you give them back sit them in the car and force feed the, 10 raspberry flavoured popsicles. *Then* shove them back in the broke whore's front door. It won't get your money back but it might make your sister start using again and make her fail her next piss test. Ha ha! Your kids are in the system now Elizabeth!

Organic. When farmers don't use spray and pesticides on the food they grow they're allowed to call that food organic and put it in special sections of the supermarket so rich people no longer have to look at the rest of us shopping - which, to be fair, is pretty gross.

People Meat.

This is a fact that many a homosexual serial killer has known for years: man is made of delicious. People are made of food. It is the best solution for the overcrowded planet. If we all eat one person over the course of the week the population halves. It deals with over crowding, hunger and the environmental cost of producing food - all in one move. So the only question left to ask is, "Do you feel like Italian or Vietnamese?" At first we'll use this new look at food to do a bit of a cull. We'll open the abattoir to the people that, if we are honest, society doesn't want. The violent criminals, drug addicts, prostitutes, child actors, bald men, spinster school teachers, people in their twenties, wearers of Oakley sunglasses and those who say "literally" literally every second word. Socially it's right. Environmentally it's right. Ethically it's... in keeping with current projections. But this should put the idea over the edge: The two most banal social media trends inflicted upon us - of photographing oneself and photographing one's meals get rolled into one and cancel each other out forever. #selfiedinner.

Queue.

There are two types of queues for food in the world. The first is where malnourished children with distended bellies and tin plates stand in line for a scoop of millet porridge. The second is where over fed western sugar junkies stand in line at Krispy Kreme waiting for hot doughnuts to come out of the fryer because NOM NOM NOM.

Rhino Horn Pasties.

Sharks fins, tiger penis, cobra eyes and leopard eyelid. What the fuck is wrong with Chinese people? Stop eating all the best animals you cunts. Your desire for a bigger hardon is decimating the Earth's wildlife. Chinese women gigantic vaginas are the biggest single cause of extinction the planet has known.

Sausages.

Abattoirs are the places where animals are processed. A pig goes in one end - a series of heinous crimes, morality swerves and corporate malfeasance takes place and then a sausage comes out the other end.

TV Chefs.

Is it just me or does Jamie Oliver look like a fat Jamie Oliver?

UA93.

The twin towers were not taken down by angry Muslim extremists as everyone likes to think. That was just the cover story sold to us by the airlines. 911 was actually caused by normal men pushed too far by the food on offer on their flights. It all started by retrieving some box cutters from their luggage to cut the crust off the mashed potatoes and once they tasted the pudding it all just kind of spiralled from there. Those men were heroes. R.I.P.

Vegan. You know how you can tell if someone's a vegan? Wait 30 seconds and they'll tell you. We could end our love affair with meat but that's called being a 'vegan' and although meat could give you cancer of the arsehole, being a vegan will turn you into an actual arsehole.

Wine. Knowing a *lot* about wine is basically like admitting that you hate black people.

Xenical. If you're obese there's a pill you can take to block the fat from the food you eat from absorbing into your system and making you even fatter. It's called Xenical. If that doesn't work there's a pill called Ambien and you take 30 of them with a bottle of vodka - and your fat days will be well and truly over.

Yellow Fin. Soon there'll be no fish in the ocean and we'll all look back and go, "Remember when we used to put tuna into cans and feed it to our cats? That shit was hilarious." And then we'll be like, "Pass the salt this tinned cat tastes terrible."

Zero Hours Contract. When you eat fast food the people that prepare it get paid nothing and are treated like modern day slaves. This is why they take all the rage, frustration and sense of injustice they have inside themselves and 'hoick' it into your hamburger. Revenge isn't just sweet - revenge is the secret in secret sauce.

HOLLY
WOOD

Apart from the Internet movies are the greatest thing humans have invented and if you don't agree then fuck you - take off your 'people suit' and fuck off back to planet cunty. Movies are how I learned about the world. Movies are how I know how to definitely diffuse a bomb on a bus travelling at 50 mph and sharks are inherently evil and that greed is good and that following your dreams is all that matters... and ghosts can do pottery. But Hollywood aint movies. Hollywood is the conditions you need to create movies. It's the primordial cordial that movies crawl out of. And even though your chances of actually making it in Hollywood as an actor are basically zero it's a town filled with people who are definitely going to make it.

Agent. Because Hollywood actors are artists (bile in mouth) not business people (pah), they need agents. We all know about agents because sometimes in movies actors play agents who are representing actors who are played by other actors... Because the whole thing is just a self fulfilling echo chamber of money and ego.

Brangelina. When you're the two biggest stars (best looking people) in Hollywood (La La land) and you get together 'everybody's talking about it'. In fact, everybody's talking about it so much that they need a way to shorten your names because it's taking so long to say Brad and Angelina so they push the two together to make one name therefore saving valuable seconds that the 'press' can use speculating on what country they'll steal their next child from (Ethiopia) or guessing what body part they'll get replaced next (eyes).

CGI. When the make-up women run out of the trailers with their hands in the air screaming about how they're not miracle workers that's when the most powerful computers man has built step in and give hope for actresses over 40.

Dog. There's a dog size to cunt ratio that Hollywood seems to operate on. If your dog fits in a handbag chances are your ego won't fit in an aircraft carrier.

E. There's a TV channel that's devoted to the lives of celebrities and actors. It's on 24 hours a day and it's brilliant... if you're filled with too much hope for the future of the human race.

Follower. Film stars used to have fans but now they have followers. Thanks to the measurability of social media, fame is now easy to equate in likes, views, comments shares and, yes, followers. And like all things shitty in the world, the people deciding on who is famous are what are called tweens. Everything tweens like is terrible because their attention span is - hey look a puppy in sunglasses. These are people who have, only just stopped sticking bits of LEGO into their vaginas and they are playing a major role in controlling our cultural landscape and that's why Selina Gomez.

Greyhound Buses. They come from all over. Iowa, Ohio, Oklahoma and other flyover shitholes with dreams of stardom and fame. They sit on the bus and head to dream-town to make it as an actor in the movies… and thanks to those who dare to dream we now all know what a pussy looks like with a fist, a bat handle and two dicks stuffed in it at all at once.

Hand Prints. If you make it as an actor you'll press your hands into concrete on Hollywood boulevard. And this will be the only time you'll ever get have to get your hands dirty again.

"**I**'d like to thank…" Actors are the most important people in the world doing the most important thing in the world. It's true - just ask other actors.

Jews. Sometimes movies like Pirates Of The Caribbean gets made and then they make a sequel and then they make a third one and a fourth and a fucking fifth and I think that maybe it's all just a plot to punish us for not coming to the rescue sooner when the Nazi's were doing their thang. In which case the debt is repaid - sure you lost 6 million people but we've had to endure Johnny Depp in a Halloween costume for a fucking decade.

Kickstarter. Independent films are films that are made outside the Hollywood system. They exist so white people can make each other look inferior and stupid by asking each other if they've seen them yet and racing each other to make the most pretentious observations - "I feel it was overly reliant on an aesthetic that hasn't been relevant since Pedro Alvaraz LaJoya made that film set entirely in a closet - 'Wardrobe'

Little People. Fame is a pyramid scheme. For every Hollywood star there are 40 million normal people fawning and worshipping him like some lame ass groveling half-humans. We all seem to believe that looking into the middle distance and saying some pretend words turns people into Demi Gods. How can they respect us when we care so much about everything they do - "Jennifer Aniston does fart with upward inflection - is her colon asking questions about recent break up?" How can they see us as real people when we subjugate ourselves to them? I'm surprised more fans aren't casually murdered by bored Hollwood elite. Those screaming fans waiting all night outside Zac Effron's hotel. Why not walk out to the balcony and drop a statue on a few?

Squish some. Put a couple in a jar and throw some fire works in with them. Tear the wings off some. Burn some to death with a magnifying glass. Fan-snuff filmed on Swarovski Crystal encrusted iPhones with the Instagram filter that makes the pink of the teenagers guts and brains POP.

Mom. Behind every successful actor… is a crazy eyed bitch forcing her kid to learn how to tap dance, annunciate and ready to burn a teddy-bear's legs off if her little pay check has to cry in an audition and (the worst) naming her kids Brittany, Megan or Ryan.

Nic Cage. What happened to you, bro? If you're reading this get in touch man. You don't have to go through… whatever it is, alone.

Out. There are no Gay actors in Hollywood there are only vagina loving leading men types. The one guy who is especially not gay is Tom Cruise. He's as heterosexual as a row of tents.

Paparazzi. Boo-hoo actor you want your life back? Oh. Life. Back. Do you mean 'real life' life. Like when you run out of toilet paper and forget to buy more for three weeks and every time you take a shit you have to shower, Mr Depp? You mean

you want to re-embrace concepts like 'Wednesday', Mr Dicaprio? You want to figure out where the weird fishy smell in your car is coming from because it's making your clothes stink and you have job interview at that printing place, Ms Johannson. Like fuck you do. You want your cake and you want to eat it… and throw it up later. But the thing is – you took the MONEY and even though you are superior to us in every way – better looking, more interesting, better dressed, travelled, fed and fucked – *we* gave you your life and *we'll* tell you when to stop dancing… Now be quiet while we jerk off to the private nude photos you emailed to your boyfriend.

Quintessence. Surely one of the strangest phenomena's is celebrity perfume. J Lo has made millions from 'JLo GLOW' flying off Wal-Mart shelves to be sprayed into the waxy crevasses of the scrotal skinned wives and mothers of Middle America. Presumably it smells like mocking irony with undertones of outright laughter and sheer amazement. *Justin Beiber – Scroat*. A zesty fragrance with notes of tragically unpunched face. *Gywneth Paltrow – Alimony*. For the lady that wants to smell like organic smugness and the tears of relief from an English songwriter.

R Kelly - Nonconsensual. A weighty cologne that makes a man smell like brandy, urine and rape kit.

Rotten **Tomato.** Not everyone can make a movie but anyone can wreck one. Word of mouth used to be what would happen when you would tell someone what you thought of something. You'd walk up to your friend and say "Transformers 5 sucks" and they might tell their friend they'd heard that "Transformer 5 sucks" it but by that time it was too late - it had already taken a gajillion dollars in box office takings in the opening weekend and the execs would be laughing, "Ha ha ha we knew it was dog shit that's why we didn't let reviewers see it." Now you can be sitting in the movies and tweet "Transformer 5 sucks" and you'll see them boarding up the cinema on the way out... Well not you - you only have 200 followers and most of them are bots trying to get you to date a MILF - but you get what I mean.

Sequel. America's favourite genre is SEQUEL. Case in point - there are seven Rocky films. He's fought everyone and everything and won. In Rocky 8 Stallone's going toe to toe with colon cancer caused by Human Growth Hormone and no one's expecting him to win this one.

3D. When you have a small, useless cock you buy a BIG car...

United **Nations.** Sometimes actors go to the UN, make their serious face and talk about issues that affect humanity. We need actors to do this because they are the only ones who are skilled enough to convincingly pretend someone actually gives a fuck about starving poor people / women.

Vampires. People love vampires because they are young, glamorous and stay good looking forever. And even though she's scary as shit - that's how we know Madonna isn't a vampire.

Waitress. In Hollywood if people tell you they are actors, screenwriters or directors and you should ask to see a dessert menu – then they'll stop bothering you for a few minutes.

Xi-Jinping. The only reason the Chinese president hasn't foreclosed on the debts that America owe them and forced the whole country into groveling servitude is that he likes seeing them Hollywood titties on the big screen. Hollywood tits were, are and will always be America's most successful peace emissary.

"Yipee Kai Yay Mother Fucker".** Great moments in cinema history No. 775: "CUT! This time try walking away from the explosion and DON'T look back over your shoulder. Just keep walking… a facial expression like you need to shit a pineapple. Got it?"

Z-List. There's a ranking that corporations have forced our culture to participate in where we rank actors and their Hollywood cohorts in our minds. Some are A list and we love them because they're 'amazing human beings'. Others are Z-list and we loathe them because we all know that they're 'vile human beings'. It might seem trivial, petty and cruel but it's important because it gives us all something to do in the minutes between meals.

Internet

Before the Internet we finished school and for the most part that was the extent of our knowledge. We might learn one or two more things ~~like~~ like a knot or two and sure, some brainiac would read some more books and find out some more here and there, but no one ~~that~~ was all clued up like now. Back in those days if you wanted to learn how to make a pipe bomb at 2am you had to find someone who knew how to make a pipe bomb at 2am and that meant walking around asking people or going to a bar. Now days just go to pipebomb.com and download the PDF and get on with your research. Or say you wanted to jerk off looking at a man fuck a child you either had to fuck the child yourself and take Polaroids or drill a hole in the wall at the back of a parish. But now anyone can jerk off to everything and all is right in the w.w.world.

Anonymous. In "Revenge Of The Nerds Part Now" the nerds are less concerned with showing the jocks who's boss and nailing some cheerleader BUSH! They're more concerned with justice, free speech and keeping the most important human invention a democratic space for the use of you, me and all the delightful German weirdos in chat rooms who want to find someone to eat their penises.

Bit Coin. In Super Mario you are a moustachioed plumber who races around collecting coins. Bling Bling Bling Blinngggggiittty Blong. Okay that's what Bit coins are… except those game coins can be used in the real world for real goods and services. Which judging by your moustache and your 'friend' Luigi will be tickets to musicals, excellent mid century Danish furniture, and some darling wrapping paper.

Cats. Approximately 33% of the entire Internet is devoted to an animal that, if it were just a couple of KGs heavier, would carry babies off into the undergrowth and eat their soft organs. Feral fucking things.

Dot Com Millionaires. Internet millionaire's are the worst millionaires. They buy normal houses wear Mom jeans and Seinfeld series 3 sneakers and marry women with real breasts. And they are single handedly putting the giant shark aquarium companies out of business. Can one of your rich wankers please run over a pregnant hooker with a Ferrari in Vegas hotel hallway up in this piece?

ESports. Meanwhile in the real world: There are 67 million monthly players on a role playing game called League Of Legends from all over the world and stadiums are being filled with cheering human fans dressed in cosplay like their favorite characters to support 'teams' of carpel-tunnel afflicted teenagers they call 'athletes' with translucent skin and breath that smells like RedBull + Cheetos and who have nappy rash from pissing themselves while they 'train' for up to 18 hours a day to become pros. And though it all seems fairly virtual, professional video gamers are making millions of real dollars a year and driving real Ferraris and beeping their real horns at their real fathers and laughing real hard.

4Chan. The real Internet isn't those perfectly designed .COMS with well thought out typefaces and worried over UX and UI and other interface acronyms. The real Internet is a string of abuse, inside jokes, trolling and pictures of old men sucking off old men for LULZ.

Google Search Page 2. This may freak you out but that row of numbers at the bottom of a Google search are OTHER PAGES of search results. I know. For the longest time I thought this is what they were talking about when they talked about the dark web. My suggestion is just get rid of it - who the fuck wants to go to a pet store that has terrible SEO anyway? That would be like using the yellow pages and dialling a plumber that starts with the letter B. I say delete all those websites and make more room for cats.

"Hashtag Just Saying." The Internet isn't just the only thing what we talk about - it's now officially how we talk.

I.R.L. If you are in a conversation that gets very boring but you can't make it stop, if you are staring at something that you can't swipe to change or the food you are looking at is actually about to go into your mouth you are probably, what they call on the Internet 'In real life'. Try not to touch anything and whatever you do don't start masturbating.

Jennifer is a fat fucking whore. By far and away the worst thing about cyber bullying is not the suicides caused by it, the lives ruined and the fact that it's growing year on year - it's those fucking stock shots you see every time some news outlet runs a story on it. They are beyond fucking depressing. If I have to see one more teenaged model showing us her acting chops by pretending to cry while looking at laptop from the 1920's I'll kill myself.

Kim's Buttocks. Breaking the Internet is when something in pop-culture is so of the moment, so right now, so shareable and so hawt that the whole of the Internet erupts with fervour about that piece of pop-gum and all the servers spew out smoke like Miley Cyrus's tour bus. It could be Taylor Swift wearing a tee shirt with an Internet meme on it, it could be a felon with piercing blue eyes and to-die-for bone structure or it could be a massive shiny pair of buttocks. These have all "Broken the Internet"

- because apparently the Internet is as durable as Paris Hilton's hymen.

Like-tivism. The revolution is a messy business. The occupy movement is a bunch of tent sniffing hippies who mean well but could easily melt your sleeping bag to your legs by dropping a fire poi on you in a sharing circle. That, and they smell like goat sex and lack a sense of humor even though they dress like medieval jesters. And the direct action, Arab springers bunch get shot a bit too often for our middle class tastes. So the best place to get involved and change the world is on the Internet. More specifically sitting on your toilet slack jawed surrounded by your own poo-ghost while pressing LIKE with your thumb. Syrian orphans? LIKE. Homeless Londoners? LIKE. Something about the Gays that you can't be bothered reading? LIKE. Now wipe your arse and stand up before your feet go numb - you've done enough changing the world for one day 'Bob Smelldoff'.

Meme. All your news feed are belong to us. Much trend. Such lazy.

North Korea. How fast do you think we'd start killing each other after money stopped coming out of the ATM's because some smart cookie sitting in an air-conditioned office with a portrait of the Dear Leader glaring down at them figured out how to wipe our bank accounts clean of money? I give it three meals or two days - whichever comes first.

Orwell. Thanks to the American hero Edward Snowden. Snowden leaked PRISM and other terrifying PowerPoint documents outlining the NSA's mass surveillance programs and revealed to the world: As we all suspected PowerPoint is inherently evil. We are governed by people who see and treat us as adversaries. They don't respect us, they don't like us and they sure as shit don't trust us. A secret obsessed government becomes a secret government and in turn we become a secret society… then a whispering society… and finally a silent one. That's why privacy is important. Because otherwise we all just shut up and all the incredibly beautiful, smart beyond reproach, hilarious, ingenious people filled with capabilities so broad and exquisite it makes me want not to kill a whole lot of you… disappear and the whole Internet becomes dark not just a corner of it.

Pornography. Women like Alexis Texas getting gang-pounded had as much to do with the creation of the Internet as Tim Berners Lee. The fact that you can stream video to your phone would still be 5 years away of it wasn't for pornography selling people the chance to jerk off in the car on the way to work. Without porn and the insatiable horniness of men the Internet would be a dial up, text only glorified calculator for nerds to send puzzles to each other with.

Quick Look. Before I write this I'll just have a quick look on the old Facebook_ _

‒ ‒ ‒ ‒ ‒ ‒ ‒ ‒ ‒ ‒ ‒ ‒ ‒ ‒
‒ ‒ ‒ ‒ ‒ ‒ ‒ ‒ ‒ ‒ ‒ ‒ ‒ ‒
‒ ‒ ‒ ‒ ‒ ‒ ‒ ‒ ‒ ‒ ‒ ‒ ‒ ‒
‒ ‒ ‒ ‒ ‒ ‒ ‒ ‒ ‒ ‒ ‒ ‒ ‒ ‒
‒ ‒ ‒ ‒ ‒ ‒ ‒ ‒ ‒ ‒ ‒ ‒ ‒ ‒
‒ ‒ ‒ ‒ ‒ ‒ ‒ ‒ ‒ ‒ ‒ ‒ ‒ ‒
‒ ‒ ‒ ‒ ‒ ‒ ‒ ‒ ‒ ‒ ‒ ‒ ‒ ‒
‒ ‒ ‒ ‒ ‒ ‒ ‒ ‒ ‒ ‒ ‒ ‒ ‒ ‒
‒ ‒ ‒ ‒ ‒ ‒ ‒ ‒ ‒ ‒ ‒ ‒ ‒ ‒
‒ ‒ ‒ ‒ ‒ ‒ ‒ ‒ ‒ ‒ ‒ ‒ ‒ ‒
‒ ‒ ‒ ‒ ‒ ‒ ‒ ‒ ‒ ‒ ‒ ‒ ‒ ‒
‒ ‒ ‒ ‒ ‒ ‒ ‒ ‒ ‒ ‒ ‒ ‒ ‒
‒ ‒ ‒ ‒ ‒ ‒ ‒ ‒ ‒ ‒ ‒ ‒ ‒ ‒
‒ ‒ ‒ ‒ ‒ ‒ ‒ ‒ ‒ ‒ ‒ ‒ ‒ ‒
‒ ‒ ‒ ‒ ‒ ‒ ‒ ‒ ‒ ‒ ‒ ‒ ‒ ‒
‒ ‒ ‒ ‒ ‒ ‒ ‒ ‒ ‒ ‒ ‒ ‒ ‒ ‒
‒ ‒ ‒ ‒ ‒ ‒ ‒ ‒ ‒ ‒ ‒ ‒ ‒ ‒
‒ ‒ ‒

Reasons Buzzfeed Lists Are Great.

1. 10 baby animals that look exactly like something better than filling in your time sheets.
2. 20 times Beyoncé wore yellow that are more exciting than talking to your husband.
3. 10 hedgehogs that are not the crushing reality of your commute home.
4. 15 cupcakes that are more life affirming than your children's whining.
5. 10 worst days Leonardo Di Caprio has ever had that are better than the one you're having now.

Silk Road. The most famous corner of the dark web. Where anyone can buy anything. And I mean anything. Including but not limited to: drugs, guns, murder, kidnap, hackers for hire, bombs and bomb making equipment, counterfeit currency, false passports, social security numbers, green cards, stolen credit card numbers, unregulated biotic materials, human organs and of course child abuse films and images. It's like digital apocalypse down there - lawless desperadoes wearing headgear adorned with bird skulls all gathered round forums and poorly designed websites like they're small tire-fires. Trading children, weapons, homicide, new identities, hints 'n' tips on mass destruction and other tomfoolery - for jewellery made from human molars... except the molars are bit coins and they're probably wearing chinos not bird skulls. Evil is always way more banal than we think.

Terabyte. The Google Indexed Internet is 200 Terabytes big. And that's only 0.004 of the total Internet. Most of the Internet is abandoned travel, fitness, and parenting blogs set up by well meaning middle class people named Barnaby who rapidly found out that turning a shitty blog into revenue stream is WAY harder than being an account manager or whatever the fuck Barnaby does and so it's better to just give up and go back to lying to people at parties bout what it is he does.

Ugandan Secretary Of Defense & Accounting. *"My Dear Friend, My name is Dr. Ben Mboye, a Uganda national. I was the Permanent Secretary of Defense & Accounting Officer in Uganda. One of my reasons for contacting you is to share my joy with you that I have been exonerated and cleared by Hon Justice Julie Sebuntinde from the probe that involves three junk Chopper Helicopter purchased from Russia. My*

second reason is to ask you about the possibility of investing in your country that I believe we can embark upon together. The money realized from the sales of my properties was added to the money that was withdrawn from my account and the total amount was US$15,500,000.00 (Fifteen Million, Five Hundred Thousand United States Dollars). Since I could not lodge this fund into any bank account for fear of being traced, the money was packaged and deposited with a Security Company that belong to a Holland national, based in South Africa for safekeeping..."

Let me stop you there, Dr. Ben. You had me at three junk chopper helicopters. Just tell me the PayPal account you need the money wired to and let's get investing!

Viral. A fat Korean man in glasses rides an invisible horse while a baby bites his brothers finger and a bulimic she-man screams at us to leave Britney alone while a double rainbow pierces the sky on the way home from the dentist and you'll never guess what happened next - RICK ASTLEY!

WIFI Code. If you came from the planet Xunumamna you'd be excused for thinking "What's your WIFI code?" is the way people greet each other on this planet.

XIf7HdU. Thanks to the gradual tech take over, now the onus is on us to prove that we are humans. We do this by typing random letters and numbers into little windows because a computer would be like, I'M A COMPUTER I'M NOT DOING THAT MENIAL SHIT – THAT'S PEOPLE WORK.

YouTube Comment. Movie idea: A serial killer reads YouTube comments and then hunts the commenters down and does to them whatever dumb threat they made in the comment thread. I'd call it Thumbs Down and post it on YouTube… the sequel would start writing itself almost immediately.

Zoe16. A great way to keep kids safe online is to make all the places they hang out online so uncool that they stop being online - Facebook used to be a pedophiles bread and butter but now it's just filled with grandparents complaining about Netflicks and posting all the same cat photos you already posted seven years ago.

People don't want justice, people want revenge. Just call it what it is and do away with the whole lawyer, trial and sentencing charade. All the courts should do is establish blame and then let the victims decide what happens to the perpetrator. But ~~this~~ it should be that whom ever chooses the punishment has to dish it out too. That's the rub. It's easy to put someone to death if you don't actually have to do it.

This would also stop the cutting off of hands/cocks/noses and because not many people can go there and the people that can are probably the ones about to get lectured/frowned at and growled to death by the rest of us.

Audience. When someone gets executed by the state, if you're a victim of the crime the person committed, you're allowed to go and watch the dude die. It's supposed to give the victims closure but I doubt the pain dies with the perpetrator of the pain. I'm sure it's just another person dead and a way for the prison system to up their revenues by selling popcorn.

Biblical. There's so much stoning in the bible it makes me think it was written by the stone masons of yore as a way to up the sales of their fist sized rocks.

Crime. When it comes to illegal shit there are some definite no-no's and then there are some judgment calls that are about your morals and principles. My view is that the things you shouldn't have to tell me not to do are crimes. No one has to tell me not to murder someone or rape someone or even take someone's bike. Let's keep it simple. If it makes someone bleed or makes someone cry it's a crime. But, to me everything else is pretty much fair game.

DNA. Listen, do what ever makes you happy and what your lack of impulse control forces you to do - but remember - you can't do anything fun without spraying at least a tea-cup full of DNA all over the place these days so take a black light with you for after you've taken all the polaroid's you need to take and you're onto the clean up.

Eye For An Eye. Ever wondered why that Lady Justice with the scales in one hand is wearing that bandage on both her eyes?

Flogging. Okay so it would hurt like shit and it cuts you down to the bone and you could die from it... but if you survive it's over quick - not like some long slow prison sentence where you have to eat empty carbs and sleep under a scratchy blanket on a bed made from amnesia foam (whatever the opposite of memory foam is).

Genocide. A crime against the whole of humanity is a pretty big crime and requires a pretty big slice of justice pie. Which is the thing about giving the death penalty to some dude who shoots his wife for example. You kill him and end his life - which is fairly ultimate. So what do you give to a General that murders a whole village of people in the name of an imaginary God? Or a president of country who uses Saran gas on his neighbours? You let him languish in a cell for years? Boring – we do that to people who get smoking weed in the wrong places. Maybe you have to kill him then bring him back and kill him again and bring him back and kill him again. Now we're talking. Over the course of a decade it's just a series of being killed and then brought back to life and nursed back to heath to be killed again. Run him over with a car – rush him to surgery. Drown him in a river – have the CPR teams waiting. Electrocute him dead and then shock him back. Maybe it's more of a kill him, resuscitate him, let him go and re assimilate into society. Maybe marry, settle down and start to lead a normal life – sign up for iCloud storage for their photos and music, get an 18-month cellphone contract and a dog then 'KNOCK KNOCK' time to die, motherfucker. For the rest of his life – and then maybe longer. When he finally dies of old-age we could download his personality, sentience and all that makes him 'him' onto a computer and then put the computer into an Internet café in the Congo where the generator periodically runs out of gas. Or maybe just stop the death penalty altogether and find a way to solve problems without death being involved – shit we might set some sort of example.

Hate Crime. If you beat someone to death while you call him a "faggot nigger Jew dyke" it's a hate crime. If you beat the dude to death and remain silent it's just a 'dislike' crime.

Insanity Plea. The difference between spending your life being a wank-mitten in a penitentiary and sitting in a mental hospital doing group therapy - smoking cigarettes and sharing tales of the subpar Christmas presents you got as a kid basically comes down to this: When did you do all the weird sex stuff? Was it *before* you murdered the woman or *after* you murdered the woman?

Judge. Most of us have got all our information on the workings of the courts from watching to movies and TV. We know all the cool stuff to say like, "Objection" when the punk ass prosecutor gets all uppity and off-piste and we know that we have to approach the bench when we pull that new evidence out of our arse and we know that any more outbursts like that and we'll be in contempt… But we also know that old man Dixon is tough but fair so we'll take our chances.

Karma. Having some despicable middle class twat who read half the Bhagavad Gita and now spends his whole time juggling detritus and wearing fisherman pants telling you his views on how we are all just energy and made from each other's reformed space dust and that life and death isn't linear and nothing ever really ends – happened to you because you're a shitty fucking person who masturbates thinking about his step sister and steals post it note pads from work. It's called Karma and it's about to tell you about its trip to Indonesia when it lived in a village and found happiness in the hearts of others.

Lynching. The thing about lynching is that you waste a lot of rope. Once you've lynched someone you have to just forget that length of rope – mainly because there's some guy tied to one end and lynching is not super-dooper legal. In the old days there was so much lynching and rope buying that there were rope-millionaires that sprung up. Of course, they couldn't come out and say – "Lynching rope for sale" because of the legal thing – they had to pretend it was for something more socially accepted… like tying your wife to a stake and beating her with a handful of willow branches for back talk.

Mob Justice. If the baying-mob comes tap-tap-tapping on your door in the middle of the night with some gasoline, baseball bats and pitch forks and you're standing there in one of your kitchens looking at the bank of CCTV cameras watching as they use your neighbours head as a door knocker you should probably know you had it coming and maybe you should have got on board with that 5% minimum wage increase you were so anti – you know, "Let them eat cake" and all that.

Neo Slavery. When you turn prisons into corporations and make inmates work for pennies a week, that's called corporate slavery. Here are just some of the companies indulging in this morally dubious practice: WHOLE FOODS, MC DONALDS, WENDY'S, WALMART, STARBUCKS, SPRINT, VERNON, FIDELITY, JC PENNY, AMERICAN AIRLINES, and in the cruellest of all 'fuck you's', VICTORIA'S SECRET. They must have to have a cum trough on the production line for all the surreptitious tearful wanking.

Out. After being treated like animals, exposed to preventable violence, neglect and dehumanising conditions, millions of people a year are freed from the confines of prison. Then it's their turn to evaluate their own personal meaning of justice and how it's handed out.

Presumption Of Innocence. One of the tenants of a decent system of Justice. You go into the court room... in street clothes because you don't have a suit... with bruises all over your face from the arrest... with the wrong coloured skin... say "ax" when you really mean "ask"... and everyone presumes you're as innocent as sin. Aint that right, Tyreek?

Quota. If you're a shit hole town in the middle of America and your abattoir just shut down maybe you can get a corporation to build you a McJail. This will guarantee jobs for your village dullards. That job will be baby sitting a bunch of rushed-through-the-system-offenders on dubious war-against-drugs charges. Meanwhile the private prisons get paid by the government who are forced to meet what they call 'lock up quotas'.

Meaning if the beds are empty the prisons get paid anyway... "So Jerome Black we find you GUILTY - now what was the charge?"

Revolving Door. You remember that show CHEERS about the bar where everyone knew your name, and they were always glad you came? There was Sammy the bartender and Norm Peterson the loveable drunk who sat on the stool night after night unable to stay away because the place was like his home. And there was Cliff the postman who finally found a modicum of respect at Cheers. Woody the young guy who made everyone sexually confused. That's like jail for some people. It's called being 'institutionalized' and prison is full of Norms... except they're not amiable fatties in corduroy jackets, they're scarred up hard men with swastikas tattooed on their foreheads and FUCK COPS tattooed on their eyelids and they know your name - your name is Shirley.

Solitary Confinement. For most of us that's when our iPhone runs out of battery halfway through the commute home.

Top Bunk. You accidentally reversed over your neighbour's lil toddler and now you have to a lil time. This is your best bet, white belly. Braid your hair, cut your jeans off into Daisy Duke shorts, make some fake tits out of balled up toilet paper and bash all your teeth out of your own mouth with a metal pipe. Now you look like a woman and your mouth has become a vagina with different tightness settings (depending on your jaw strength). Look, you're going to have to have sex with men why get the shit beat out of yourself every time it happens as well? Just lean into your new role and maybe when you get out in 12 years you'll be a little more understanding of some of the things your wife has to go through.

U W R K F R E E. Getting inmates making license plates, picking up trash or paving roads for free while they're in jail isn't necessarily a bad thing except when you see who most of the inmates are and who put them there. Then those license plates start looking a shit load like cotton bushes.

Vigilante. Due process, lawyers, courtrooms and judges are a fucking drag. You know what else is a drag? The guilty dude we tied to the bumper of our pick up truck about 3 miles back.

Wrongfully. Ouch. That's a bittersweet word to hear after you've spent half your life in the system. On one hand it means you get out of jail on the other hand your other hand is clenched up into a fist so tight and angry it's turning your nails into little hate diamonds.

Xicano. The thing about coming from a shit hole of a country like Mexico where everyone is poor, murder rates are in the 10's of thousands a month and your beer tastes like it's already been drunk once, is that Jail is an improvement not a punishment.

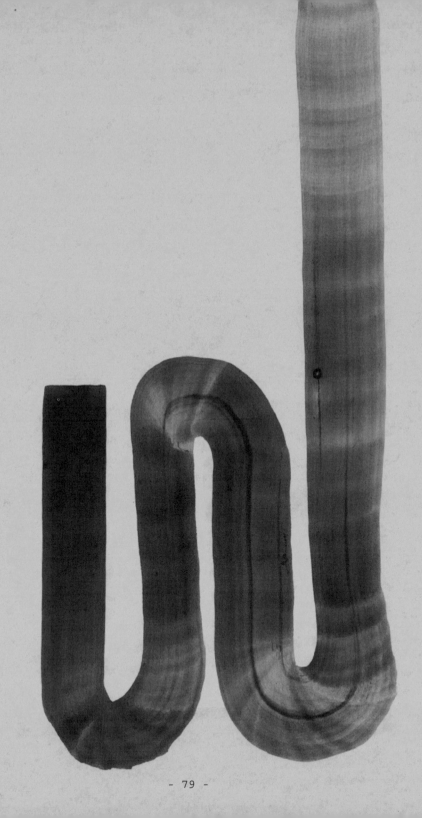

When you're a collector of things and what you
discover is the more rare that thing
is the more valuable it is. With this fact
in mind: The world is fucking drowning
in people. There are 7 billion of us on
this rock. By far and away one of the
most populous large mammal out here
and still we believe two things.
1. Human life is valuable (pah) and
2. It's somehow our birthright to
have kids. Kids were a necessity back
in the day. People used vaginas to create
a little work force and they had to keep
having more kids incase some of the
work force stopped showing up for work/
died of polio. But now Chinese people do
all the work so the rest of us have kids
as a vanity project of which the highlight
seems to be naming them and dressing them
them. It's shameful just how vain we have
become. The only good news is that none of
this crop of children will make it
out of their 30's before the water
wars start, the cholera takes hold
and the street dogs that feast on
the carcasses of vain peoples children
take over as the most populous
mammal on the planet.

Adoption. An option, yes. But remember the older they are the less likely someone is to take them off your hands. So you'd better put your baby on a list now and move on with your 'life.'

Boredom. Nothing prepares you for the mind removing boredom you are about to face. It's just day after day of keeping a baby alive with no reprieve. The decent thing to do is suffer in silence remember this was your shitty life choice - not ours.

Cute. Perhaps nature's greatest trick. Cuteness is a baby's best natural defence against being put outside with the recycling every week and the reason very few blind people bother having kids.

Dreadlocks. Idiot adults are just fucked up kids a few years later. Something happened to that adult man twirling fire sticks at a music festival that can't now unhappen. Something terrible was done to him as a child to make that adult think it is okay for a white man to have dreadlocks. By all means approach him and open hand slap him with sickening force and repetition but that will only serve to make you and anyone watching feel better about the situation. It won't change who he is because the damage is done and society has to now deal with this know-nothing prick with a "yellow aura" and 85 pockets on his trousers. Another jerk on the jerk pile waiting for gasoline and a match.

Empty Nest. This becomes your goal. To get the kids you once thought you wanted, out of your house. To palm them off on the world and go on a holiday. This is why you see happy old people on boats in stock photos.

Family. What you now are. A family. One of those entities that are constantly annoying the rest of us while we try to eat, making the roads ugly with your utility-based vehicle choices and forcing politicians to make lame policy decisions based on your 'values'. You also make 80% of movies suck and 100% of public swimming pools a public health risk.

Go-Pro. There are lots of kids on Facebook now and they are, without exception, all very dull. Not their fault, it's just that they are kids and kids are like short films - great if they're yours, no character development and crappy dialogue if they're not. So here's a tip: A great way of making your child more exciting is to put a GO-PRO camera on it. It seems to work for every other boring thing in the world from kite surfing to record scratching. Put the GO-PRO on 'Jasper', 'Plumb', 'Bookcase' or whatever vanity plate you've stuck on the poor wee child and let it toddler about on a building site, a road, through a horse race or a crack den.

Happy Meal. All that nonsense about eating organic and your child eating what you eat will be the first thing to fly out the window. Kids don't dig shitake. You know what they say, Happy Meal, happy baby.

In-Laws. The baby sitters you don't really have to even give a shit about getting home on time for. And they're free. You never really saw the point of them until now. Before your baby they were just people you had search the bargain bins for gifts at Christmas time and a reason to get drunk well before the turkey came out.

Jasper's Mommy. Jasper, Sebastian, Felix, Arabella, Matilda…These pretentious names herald the arrival of some total asshole parent who knows what Kale is and how to prepare it.

Kindergarten. Leaving your child at kindergarten for the first time is a heady mix of joy and worry. Like, you're worried you won't be sober in time to drive the car to pick the little cunt up at 2pm.

LEGO. If you can't find a piece of LEGO turn the lights off and walk around in bare feet. Also can be located inside the nearest tiny vagina.

Moolah. A thing other people have to buy shoes and go on holidays now a thing to say out loud if you feel like and argument with your partner.

Nanny. Something both you and your husband can agree on. You both think bringing another woman into your relationship would spice things up.

Organ Farm. There are two happy moments in the parents of twins lives. When they find out they're gonna have twins and when they find out their gonna need to have to have a kidney transplant.

Pedophile. Candy and toys are expensive and children don't seem to shut up about them. Pedophiles will often give candy and gifts to children in the grooming stage of the relationship, which can represent a saving to you... Just know when to step in and intervene. Hand holding and finger sucking is probably about the right time to put some boundaries up.

Quiet. In space no one can hear your toddler scream... But you're not in space you're in a car, a bathroom, a mall, a movie, a doctors office, economy class cabin...

Ritalin. Best smoked over a sheet of tinfoil or sold outside a school gate to twitchy junkies for latte money.

Sex. This is what got you into this mess in the first place. Sex now is something only seen as a quiz in the magazines you read at the pediatrician's office.

Tantrums. Nature's birth control. One well-placed tantrum will stop not just you but anyone in earshot from considering children for the foreseeable.

Ungrateful. You'll raise them. You'll sacrifice. You'll love them. You'll keep them alive... For years you'll struggle. And in return you'll get a sullen, entitled teenager and money missing from your purse.

Village. They say: "It takes a village to raise a child." How do you choose the right village to leave your child with - and what if that village won't take your child? You could just leave your child outside the village and run away but most village-people are excellent trackers and will know the surrounding terrain better than you so they'll probably catch you. No. The answer is - you'll have to raise the child yourself. You're going to have do a decent job too - you have to give a child a childhood that was a step up from yours and try not to add another jerkoff adult to the pile of human fuckwits we all have to clamber over everyday all day

Why? The question you will be asked constantly by a little voice... not the one from your child - the voice that lives in your head. As in, "Why, why, why did you do this to yourself?"

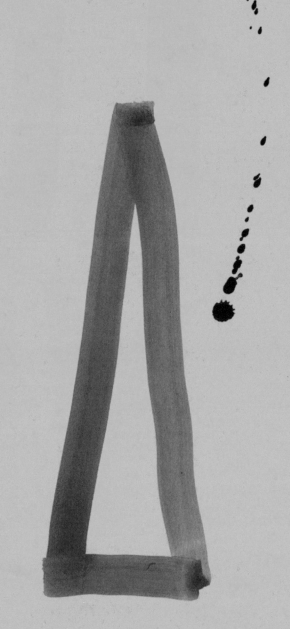

The albatross mates for life. We all learnt this from a movie where two people were in love. Movie love is the best love and, thanks to movies, it's the love people think all love should be like. Fucking bullshit. Love is not pop-bang-boom fireworks it's shovel-scrape-dig road works. It's mundane as shit and its only real purpose in being the thing ~~thing~~ that tips the balance and stops you from ~~wondering~~ murdering a perfectly good wife on a Saturday morning in a shopping mall. Not because you're angry and full of hate but because you're irritated and full of latte. Right before you lash out and hit her with your baby by swinging it by the legs like a mace the love kicks in and you just go into middle distance shut down, stop being an obstinate, cheap prick and put $50.00 pillow freshening spray in the shopping trolley.

Alone. You start this way and you will die this way and the most you can hope for is to share the middle part with someone who makes you laugh, ignores your nose picking and doesn't embarrass you in front of your work friends.

Blood Diamonds. Your loving relationship is a fantastic opportunity to win yet another competition and rub the world's face in your relative success. It's time to show the world how God-damn stinking-in-love you are and how much more love your love is worth than the your friends and colleagues. It works like this: The bigger the piece of finger carbon you have the better your love is compared to the other people out there that are just in love but don't have any glittering proof on their claws. They say they're in love but where's the proof? Do you love each other enough to die for each other? Of course not but the diamond of your ring lets the world know that you love each other enough to let a 13-year-old African kid die for you.

Couple. There goes your individual identity. You went from being a semi-interesting human with the chance of having an original thought in your own head and a life that's yours, to choosing to divide every opinion, experience, dollar and idea in half until you're just a lukewarm, nodding gibbon looking to your partner for assurance that you're still towing the line and saying the right thing.

Divorce. Guys, instead of getting married why not just find someone you think is a poisonous troll and give them a most of your money every month.

Erectile Dysfunction. Here's the thing: If you wake up in the morning with a hard on but when you go to bed at night you can't get one - you don't have a problem with your penis, you have a problem with her vagina.

Flowers. Oh dear Darren, what have you done this time?

Grindr. Invented by gays because walking into a bar and putting your dick through a hole in the toilet stall wasn't easy enough. Currently over 9 million users and 10,000 horny homos joining daily and all spending an hour on the app per day. Now, thanks to technology, you reach into your pocket, you push a button, and you can have sex with a stranger. The only way I, as a heterosexual male that isn't a rockstar, can do that is if the thing in my pocket is a switch-blade and the button I push makes the blade come flying out.

Hello, I love you. Don't confuse the feeling of love at first sight with the feeling of ecstasy tablets or you could wake up with someone who has one dread-lock, can juggle and has a tattoo of a dolphin leaping over a ying-yang on their lower back.

It's complicated. When one person *really really* likes someone but the other person *really really* likes calling her at 4am because he's high and drunk and wants to have sex with her... from behind... it's actually very, very un-complicated.

Jimmy. You meet someone, have sex with them and then get to know them. In that order. But because you're in 'lie your fucking arse off' mode and trying not to let on that you're a dirt bag who'd fuck your own cous-in, you use a condom for the first three times and... then the fourth time you go in bareback anyway. So what's the point? Girls make guys wear condoms to make guys think they aren't sluts straight out the gate and guys wear condoms so girls think that they wear them all the time and the fourth episode when they fuck with-out a condom, the dude won't be splashing an egg cup full of VD-soup on their cervix. Condoms are a joke.

Kelvey Welvin. God sent herpes to earth to punish us for our sickening baby talk and cutey pie names, Kelvin. Tell that to Jenny-wennifer.

Lust. When relationships start out, it's mostly about sex. You just want to fuck, fuck fuck. This, of course, won't last, it's just na-ture tricking you into going halves on a bookcase with a Swedish name and getting some friends that you can both share/tolerate. Honest-ly - you should masturbate before you go on any date - you'll see your date for the person they really are which is 'just another person' and it'll stop you spending your precious Saturdays walking around with someone hand in your hand trying to find the 'perfect brunch spot'.

Monogamy. "Hello, wel-come to Monogamy, we have your usual table right here. Tonight on the menu we have mince. Mince any way you like, but mince. Always mince. Mince on toast. Mince in a burrito. Mince with tomato sauce. Mince Chef will even prepare Bolognese for you. Chicken? No sir. Just mince. Mince now. Mince tomorrow. Mince forever. Mince."

Naughty Knickers. Another milestone in any relationship is when the G-stings disappear and the big-pants turn up. It's at this point if you're a man you can hold her under the blankets while you fart, tell her what you really think about her friends and making her pay for the drugs occasionally.

Over It. Breaking up is a terrible heart wrenching ordeal that makes you wish you'd never been born and makes every day feel like your heart is being dragged behind a really fast horse… A great way to get deal with a break up is to replace the person that was in your life with drugs, alcohol and the smorgasbord of strangers genitalia that you've been avoiding for the last however long – but do spare a thought for the person you've just dumped.

Passion Crime. Love means never having to say you're sorry… but so does murder.

Queef. Sometimes it's hard to know when to take the next step in a relationship: when her vagina makes that fart noise during sex and you stop pretending it didn't and laugh together – that's the moment you go get your toothbrush and move in.

Rom Com. Oh no, Susan you should totally wait for an English guy to crash his limousine into your car and then start the whirlwind romance. Who cares if his stuffy family don't like you – listen to your hilarious gay best friend that you nearly ditched for the English bloke and just be yourself… also, surprise you're a twin!

Sex Addiction. Sex addicts burst on the scene a few years ago in large part due to the availability of Internet porn. Sex addicts aren't addicted to having sex with their spouses they are addicted to easy sex – prostitutes, porn, Australian girls. But sex was never supposed to be easy to get. We were supposed to work for it. Sex is a powerful and wonderful dynamic because it is withheld. The sex dynamic twas ever thus: men want sex – women withhold it – men become better people in order to get it. When a woman holds out, a man stops acting like a fucking moron and starts stringing sentences together and using the toilet like a big boy and this gets him his reward. Okay a very simplistic view of things – but true nonetheless. EG: The second World War was won by a bunch of virgins trying to make sure there were some women left to fiddle with in their home countries. As Aristotle said, "Without beautiful women, there would be no need for money." And then he went and had sex with a boy in a Gymnasium because presumably he was broke.

Tinder. Hook up apps work great in the Gay community because before hook-up apps guys were meeting in parks to fuck each other in the buttholes without condoms while other dudes stood around and jerked off onto the dry leaves. But when straight people try and do the 'no strings sex' thing it just ends in a bunch of super awkward date rape.

Unrequited. They say they don't love you back but we both know that's not true. They do love you back, they just need to be reminded by having you follow them around, call them every hour on the hour, text them photos of the little cuts you make in your thigh to show you care and break in to their house so you can stand next to the their bed while they sleep.

Vows. It used to be that we would get married and then have sex for the first time. Now we get married and have sex for the last time.

Workplace Affairs. 85% of all affairs begin in the workplace. It could be because...
A. People dress nice at work.
B. Acronyms make panties puddle.
C. Nothing makes you feel like boning like doing a month of time sheets.
D. The provocative way you hold the white board pen when you explain your ideas for streamlining.
E. None of the above - we all work way too fucking much.

X-files. Aka Facebook after 3 glasses of wine.

YoumotherfuckerIhateyou!! It all starts with yelling it from a mountain-top and it all ends with yelling outside a nightclub.

Zygote. If your relationship is in trouble a great way to save it is to have a baby. Babies are super easy, unstressful, make women's bodies look awesome for months after the birth, bring sex back into your lives and show men for the helpful, cooperative unselfish people they are.

What the fuck is dancing? It's a weird compulsion that we have to move ourselves rhythmically (or not if you're a father). It's a very specific feeling that comes over a being and almost requires a response of limb flailing, shuffling, clapping and making the same face you make when you're fucking/ being fucked. The dancing part is just a symptom however. The cause of this oddly awesome phenomenon of dancing, is music. A kind of otherworldly language that some humans have the ability to conjure out of their beings and push through 'instruments' which are ingenious devices made at great effort, and expense to match the musician's particular interior haunting. The sound that these haunted people with their brass, wood, electric, reed, skinned, bell, steel, chain driven, amplified, stringed interpretation machines make is really often the only thing that describes the intensity of the human spirit and experience... Music is without a doubt one of the most potent proofs that human beings are exceptional animals and worthy of the esteem that we place on ourselves - even if most musicians started out doing it so they could fuck people better looking than themselves.

Auto Tune. There's a machine that can make anyone with a voice into a singer… sort of. It actually sounds like a robot wolf calling for his friends to come and feed on the carcass of what used to be pop music.

Butts. Female recording artists seem to walk into rooms and onto stage backwards and delegate the writing of lyrics and performing of music to their arses because feminism.

Clippers. Remember in the Truman show, when he gained sentience, busted through the door in the sky? Brittany Spears did the same thing when she swallowed a handful of oxy, got into her 4WD and drove to the downtown barber shop and shaved her head while being goaded by a legion of paparazzi. That was the greatest moment in pop culture history. It trumped Thriller, We Are The World and Queen at LIVE AID and Why? Because we did that. We made that happen! It was a shared effort that bullied, pushed, prodded and poked with the shit-covered stick called magazines. We made that sweet but dumb girl snap and that's the closest to having a hand in the culture we'll ever get.

Drummers. It's not true that drummers are the dumb ones of the band. Apparently it was a rumour started by drummers… wait.

Eminem. Oh awesome an Eminem song just came on at a party… 5,4,3,2,1 yep there he is. The white guy rapping along to it. "He likes spaghetti… dinner on his spaghetti… mom's all ready… mom is spaghetti." All White Males have at some point gone through a phase of liking the Rapptiy music of the ethnic people. A White Male will be able to rap the entirety of at least 3 rap songs to you at full volume with accompanying hand gestures. Not only will he be able to - but he will be COMPELLED to. If one of the 3 songs he knows comes on the stereo he will stop having an 'opinion' about whatever it is he is having his 'opinion' on and begin to rap. He won't care that you and the surrounding people are finding this uncomfortable (you may cringe so hard your vagina swallows you or if you are a dude you may simply turn inside out and your skeleton might run away). Also he won't notice that he is spilling his craft beer all over your blazer as he uses the bottle as a mic - as he 'spits' "I'm on the mic". This is a great time for one of the group to excuse himself to the toilet another to get a beer from the kitchen and another to hear their car alarm going off. However do not all leave as the White Male is prone to sulking and may simply tuck his shirt in and be a wet faced bitch for the remainder of the evening. The White Male will use the N-word as it appears in the verses and will do so ironically like an art student uses 'paint'. In the White Males mind the use of this racial slur proves that he himself is not racist. Therein the irony. However the White Male will choose to soften the use of the N word by putting the politically correct "AH" ending to the word and not the more historically accurate 'ER'. The 'AH' on the end of the N Word making it feel more like the White Male is yelling out "Surprise" from behind the couch at a super fun surprise party than yelling "Get that niggER'"out the window of a pick up truck holding a pick axe handle and a rope. Also the White Male will always, no matter how drunk, do the black-people head swivel and scan the area for someone who may take offence (also see retarded person head swivel, ginger person head swivel, homosexual person head swivel). However any lyrics about 'bitches' will just be blurted out as is because "bitches aint nothing but ho's and tricks"... everyone knows that. Some White Males may also have the Ragamuffin stylee in their repertoire and they WILL inflict that on anyone in earshot while making their hands into little pink guns "Lickashotmyselecta!" Upon finishing the ENTIRE rap song they will want some sort of praise and acknowledgement. This is an excellent opportunity for you to execute the 'Hist Fump'. (AKA 'Punching the Trout'). The 'Hist Fump' is a greeting between two white males where one of the white males goes for the High Five and the other male attempts the Fist Bump. The resulting awkward collision of appropriated handshakes is the 'Hist Fump' or the 'Trout Punch'. Look for it at your nearest sporting contest, gym or guy guy girl threesome.) The white male will also be a bit puffed out and clammy and, if over 35-years old, will generally need a sit down on the 'sofa' in the 'lounge'. Give the White Male a minute and he'll back to the conversation with his helpful opinions and views on Gaza and why Shiraz is a shit wine.

Festivals. It's all fun and games until your drugs run out then it's uncannily like you're wet, standing in a field watching other people have fun while some song you once liked plays somewhere off in the distance and you feel the thrush from that muddy fingering starting to take hold in your vagina.

Garage. It used to be that you'd start a band and play shitty music and write terrible songs for a while and then you'd start to get better because you worked at it and people would start to like your music and you'd get a gig and lose a drummer and get a better drummer then you'd get famous after a really long time of not being famous but at the route of it all was the ability to, I dunno, play a fucking instrument. Now you put on some clothes, tell the world you like Rhianna get on a stage cry, do karaoke, 'really want it', weave in an abuse narrative and boom - fame visits you like your Mother's Brother in the middle of the night when you were a little girl.

High. The war on drugs is also the war on good music.

iTunes. When you're old (anything over 14) you start becoming culturally complacent. This is because you're fucking irrelevant and your opinions on music are gross - so why bother? That's why Steve Jobs invented iTunes. A place where you and the rest of the nerd herd buy music because you're too much of a scared bitch to get it for free off the Internet. It's basically a portal for the collection of old-cunt tax.

Jazz. Don't even try to clean your house listening to Jazz. It can't be done.

'**K**illt'. You're nobody - til somebody kills you. Biggie was 'killt' by off duty cops at the behest of Suge Knight and Tupac is still alive and living on a dairy farm in New Zealand just waiting for the right time for Drake to shut the fuck up for 10 seconds so he can make his come back.

Lip Synch. Janice Joplin is dead and these days no one wants to buy music from ugly people.

Musical Theatre. Broadway in NY and Piccadilly Circus in London are what happens when middle-aged, homo song-writers do something nice for their mothers.

Napster. Started in 1999 by Sean Parker, now chair-man of Facebook, Napster was a peer-2-peer file shar-ing site primarily used for sharing music files but then it morphed in into a web-site that used the latest MP3 technology to reveal 'anti establishment rock n rollers' as the soft bellied multi-millionaire-suit-fucks that they were all along.

Ooonst Ooonst Ooonst. Even though it started in Chica-go, house music is not for Americans. Americans call it EDM (Electronic Dance Music) and play it to over-mus-cled preening fuck-boys and fake titted human blowjob machines at Las Vegas pool parties. It's not for that. House music isn't about sex – house music is about house music…

Party. It's not known which came first music or partying, but anthropolo-gists believe that which ever came first, drugs were about 2.7 seconds behind.

Quiet. If it's too loud, you're too old… Or maybe you're a newborn baby. Go the fuck home small, help-less baby. You're bumming everyone at the rave the fuck out.

Rider. When you're in a band it's hard to know if you're any good. You could listen to your fans but they probably just like your haircuts and shoes. It used to be that you'd sell a whole lot of records but now you have to give your music away or people just steal it so that's no measure ei-ther. The best way to fig-ure out if you're any good is to base it on your rider. If you go into your dress-ing room and it looks like someone set up a whole foods / liquor store in there – congrats you've made it. If you open your dressing room door and there's a fold out table with 4 warm beers and a bucket of KFC chick-en… skin on it, don't worry 'Gwen Steffani and No Doubt' – come backs can be tough.

Solo. Over the course of the 2-hour concert at least 40 minutes are solos. The Guitarist, the bassist and the drummer all get a chance to show their chops IE: wig-gle their fingers around on their instruments and make that 'I'm taking the best shit ever' face. As an audience we are supposed to look at the soloist and respond with a "I'm taking a very good shit also" face. Which is why punk music fuckin' rules. The songs are 2 minutes long and dudes in punk bands know solos are for fags in wigs.

Twenty Seven. In the past our rock stars were polite enough to live chaotic and drug addled lives and then leave the party before they started getting all pathetic and hitting their spiritual materialist phase. At 27, they'd die in their own vomit and we'd be left with the shining young God image to worship for eternity instead of some old guy wearing a bandana and orthopaedic insoles on a giant fucking stage whining about not being able to get any satisfaction.

Underground. When music is shit and the band playing it can't write a song with a hook, melody or chorus, it's not called shit, it's called 'underground'.

Vinyl. You say, "I, like, only listen to vinyl." We think, "How do I make this 50 year old virgin shut up?"

White Album. Are you a John person or a Paul person? It's basically a music nerds way of asking you if you like dogs or cats.

Xylophone. Never in the history of music has the xylophone player ever got laid. It's like the opposite of pussy. Why anyone ever learns or practices or owns a xylophone is beyond me. Even obo players are like, "Dude. Bing -bong -bing - bing...Really?"

Yodelling. If you were born in Switzerland you might get home from work, pour yourself a scotch, slip into your Eames recliner, put your headphones on and listen to some goofy fuck in leather short-veralls and little hat howling like a stabbed dog with some L's and D's chucked in for good measure. That's because music is a reflection of the culture and apparently your Switzer-culture is really really really really silly.

Zigga Zig Ahhh. Girl bands aren't really bands because they don't play music. They're just an assembly of tits and lips. Like a salad made of semi-consensual sex.

While some people are born in
Paris Hit Hilton's mother's vagina,
some people are born in Syria.
It's random as shit but one outcome
means you live in America and
have more than everything and
the other means you might die
crossing the Mediterranean in
a dinghy escaping a hell on earth
to try and eek out some decent
years as an alive person. Flags
are dumb and those who wave
them are dangerous. Borders are
arbitrary and those that defend
them are dangerous. We're all
immigrants some of us just choose
to forget because they're despicable,
selfish human trash named
Donald Trump.

America. The only country to get it's own section in this compendium *(See front of book)* for the most obvious reason of being the most culturally significant, violent, greatest, meanest, fun, free, locked up, crazy, democratic corporate dictatorship the world has ever known... for the next decade... After that it's curtains, ruin, martial law, cannibalism, celebrity rape and strewn body parts.

Brazil. They invented hairless vaginas but their police round up and murder a lot of street children because they bother tourists. So at this point you're probably with me in thinking they're breaking about even. But then you're reminded about the fact that some Brazilian monster taught Capoeira to all those middle class white guys from drum circles and you sincerely hope a monkey virus wipes out the whole fucking lot of them.

Canada. Seriously? Honestly? Who fucking cares? Find me one person who gives a shit and I'll write something here.

Denmark. These Scando countries have kept awfully quiet haven't they? You never hear about them in the news. Probably because the news is mostly terrible fucking news and it seems like these Viking motherfuckers have got bugger all of that. They're all basically socialists. High tax, free health care, free education and some sort of breeding program where only the most beautiful amongst them are allowed to further the race. Sure it's cold in the winter but the summers are these incredible 23 hour days where the Sun shines and the Danes sail little boats through archipelagos and have (free) educated conversations and drink to each others, good (free) health and then make love to each other, naked and perfect, on the grasses of glorious islands... But before you get all excited, they have a protectionist view of immigration and only let twelve people a year emigrate there so put your dick back in your pants and your passport back in the drawer you uneducated, sick, snaggle toothed fuck.

Ethiopia. Thanks to Ethiopia, every time there's a natural disaster or some poor people struggling somewhere, all the fame hungry, washed up, rock stars get together and sing a hurriedly penned sentimental ditty that we all have to do our best to ignore for about two weeks. Thanks Ethiopia - you might have flies in your eyes but we're the ones with shit in our ears.

France. You should see the fuckers put up a fight when someone suggests a 40 hour work week but invade their country and it's all "We surrender. Take our women just please don't bomb our buildings."

Germany. When you absolutely positively need to kill everyone on a continent these are the people you call. These guys are the Winston Wolf of killing innocents. It's hard to shake that little blip in the history of humanity isn't it? No matter how hip, urban, Berlinish and art based you become every time people hear your accent the first they think is - "Velcome to Auschwitz. You look tired after your train ride. How about a nice hot shower?"

Holland. Holland has the lowest crime rates in Europe. Their secret? Make everything that was illegal, legal. No crime.

Iraq. You hear about those burglars that go into peoples homes, steal everything and take a shit on the couch. I'm looking at you Cheney.

Japan. I honestly believe everyone has been looking for aliens in the wrong place. They're not in outer space. They're living in plain sight on an island in the Pacific. The Japanese are a species unto themselves - they are just so very… weird. In just one average Japanese teenagers mind lurks the thoughts of the entire dark web and all those creatures in the blackness of the deepest parts of the sea but with peoples genitals on them. Manga, eating live octopus, clubs where lost men fondle prostitutes in replica trains, those game shows that ritualize humiliation, an obsession with American culture even though America unleashed two types of hell on them for shits and giggles (the war was won you fucking Yankee sadists). Obsession with discipline, and honour slowly spoiling into repression and lost youth. A couple of decades making everything better than everyone and becoming synonymous with ingenuity and smarts. Martial arts, Ninjas and old men who force karate kids to wax their cars. Japan you whale killing freaks. You meticulous, Zen, strange, rock-a-billy, hairy bushed, karaoke bar dwelling, radiation leaking, dolphin slaying, toy collecting, wanking to comics, giggling, peace sign flashing, doll dressing up like, kamikaze, perverted, beautiful slanty-eyed aliens. I wanna build glass dome over you and turn you into a terrarium and just watch you weird-the-fuck-out until your neon burns out, all the Pokemon are caught or the World ends - which ever comes first.

Korea. There are two Koreas. One of them is a place where brainwashed citizens live in a totalitarian hell. A place where images of The Dear Leader scowl at them from every flat surface and the outside world is continually sold to them as an evil conspiracy out to get them. And other is a place where brainwashed citizens live in a consumer hell. Plastic faced K-Pop celebrities leer off every flat surface and the outside world is continually sold to them… on their credit cards. North Korea is bad - almost comically bad - unless Seth Rogan and James Franco make a movie about it and then it's un-comically bad. But South Korea is bad in a different way. Suicide represents the fourth leading cause of death in the country with about 40 South Koreans killing themselves every day. That's the highest suicide rate in the world amongst developed nations. Seoul has a bridge where hundreds of people have leapt to their end. They call it The Bridge Of Death. Very melodramatic. Causes vary but here's a clue: South Korea have what's known as a Shame Society where the main way to keep social order is through embarrassing the shit out of someone and making sure everyone you know is sitting cross legged in the shame circle too. This means people tend to bottle all of themselves up into a tight little ball of fear and then when they lose their job or fail an exam or get booted off a reality TV show - they hang them selves in the toilet while on the reality show (true story) or head over to The Bridge Of Death and chuck themselves off it. Meanwhile in North Korea suicide is apparently quite rare. Not because it's peach cobbler night every night and Mondays have been banished, but mainly because suicide is considered traitorous and the families of people who dare offend The Dear Leader by topping themselves are often punished for the crime for three generations. Which apparently is a better deterrent than renaming a suicide bridge

The Bridge Of Life and putting some motion sensors on it that trigger lights with uplifting messages when the sense someone about to end a shame spiral... which is what they did in the South.

Liberia. You'd think that giving a child a loaded AK47 would stop that child from suffering any child abuse at all - but actually it's quite the opposite.

Monaco. The Principality of Monaco is a playground for the rich. Full of upscale gambling joints and Louis Vuitton stores on every corner where there should be 7/11s. It's most famous for the high profile Monaco Grand Prix. Official population is only around 38,000 people but that number swells to around 1.5 million during the Monaco GP with the influx of 1,499,800 gold digging whores.

New Zealand. New Zealand is great at two things. Playing rugby and being a really good backdrop for movies that kids and nerds like. But let's talk about Rugby because the whole of New Zealand is. It's not an understatement to say that New Zealand's obsession with Rugby is bordering on fucking lame. When the All Blacks lose governments topple and every time there's a silence anywhere someone will fill it with some observation about 'the game'. Every ad on the television has an All Black in it (Kick your incontinence into touch with Drippy Mom Diapers). The captain could fuck any woman in the country and the coach hasn't bought a beer for 6 years. Meanwhile... The whole place is slowly being bought up by Chinese mega-rich and the white people there will soon know what the indigenous Maori people have been talking about for the last 100 years when they said - "you stole our country... " What else? Umm, Their Navy is a fishing boat with a .22 duct taped to the bow, you can drink the water out of the taps, the dudes are basic as shit and the girls finish every sentence with upward inflections and have upside down legs. (Rugby!)

Outerspace. Before we go off to colonize Mars it's worth remembering that *we already live* on a space rock that's hurtling through the vastness of the cosmos and the one we're on has cool stuff on it like seahorses and ferns. So stop being a bunch of spoilt rich second wives who are bored of their wardrobes and start figuring out how to live on Earth.

Pakistan. Twins are made when one zygote splits and turns into two embryos. Generally the result is two identical humans. But in some cases, after the split one twin gets all weird, extremist, violent, tribal, has a shitty attitude (again) to women, aides terrorism, has a nuclear arsenal and hides Osama Bin laden inside themselves.

Qatar. Built out of the desert by indentured slaves. A place where no human being goes outside for more than the time it takes to walk from the car to the mall. It's not Earth, it's planet Sand. No one could live there without air conditioning and it's one of those screwy religious time warps where Gay people get put in jail and women are treated like they're always about to do something wrong. The only good thing about it is that the official airline is Air Qatar, which is also the official musical instrument of drunken dudes when ACDC comes on the stereo.

Russia. Russians are the toughest motherfuckers on the planet. A nation of bouncers. It's like a whole country filled with shaven head hard men. Even the women and baby girls are tough hard-men. The thing about Russians is that they don't seem to give a flying, Bolshevik fuck about Russians. They love Russia. But Russians are just cogs in a human experiment that they lost the instructions to years ago. Everything about them is hardened. Their art is so sickle and hammer filled it bruises the eye, their books are so massive they give people carpel tunnel syndrome, their leaders are either riding round on horses carrying a gun with no shirt on or ordering the death of millions and ruining moustaches forever in the process. They get 100 years of industrialisation done in a decade by doing away with cement and just grinding up peoples' bones to make factory bricks. They go through the bloody political upheaval of hosting at least three 'isms' in 50 years. Their gangsters have the best tattoos and own the best hydroelectric power stations and iron ore mines. They straight-up murder denim, drink straight vodka like it's Gatorade, remove their own sense of humour with a WW2 bayonet at the age of 11, their women will fuck for fresh bread, they've cheated in every single Olympic games ever, stolen Liam Neeson's daughter, like, 3 times, they hunt homosexuals in the street with bats for sport and put punk bands in jail. And I don't even think they have a national tourism board and if they do they certainly don't have a slogan... So here you go you crazy, crazy, tough faced, ice-blooded Bolshevik capitalists: RUSSIA. FUCK YOU. FUCK OFF.

Saudi Arabia. Some mega rich guys buy a football team, a race horse or a Formula 1 car as a hobby. The rich guys in Saudi Arabia buy Jihadists.

Tuvalu. I like Kevin Costner. He's like an expensive Dennis Quad. The other thing that was expensive was that movie 'Water World'. A movie where Kev played some sort of Mad-Max on a boat that was set after the polar ice caps melted and the whole world was covered in water. What will they think of next? Kerrazy! The movie didn't do well globally except in Tuvalu. A tiny island in the Pacific, which will be the first country to disappear under the waves due to climate change. The Tuvalese fucking loved it. They loved it so much the whole island does spontaneous reenactments every time the tide come in.

UK. The UK is a cluster of some wet, cold, grim, and bleak countries comprising of Northern Ireland, Scotland, Wales and England and London. Northern Island is a country known for a GDP primarily built on the production and sale of balaclavas. Scotland is where Mel Gibson slaughtered 1000's of Jews on horseback. Wales is where Tom Jones first started backhanding hysterical woman and England used to own most of the world and is the reason we all have to fill in forms and now speak 'American'.

Venezuela. When Hugo Chavez kicked all the American interests out of Venezuela and repatriated their resources the Bush administration labeled him as 'crazy'. When Hugo Chavez started appearing on state television for 8 hours in one stretch ranting like a coked up real estate agent at his less successful cousins BBQ the rest of us kind of agreed.

Wallis and Futuna. What country do you go to if you're a Mexican, you murder someone and can't run away to Mexico?

X **Marks Your Spot.** Starting your own country is easier than it sounds, people do it all the time. They're called Micro-nations and although they're not officially recognised by any governing bodies they do give you a chance to create your very own utopia. The late Michael Jackson created a Micro-nation where he was King. The King Of Pop ruled over 'Neverland' which was a place filled with laughter and rides where the only laws were:

1. *Fun is compulsory* and
2. *The age of consent is, like, 11.*

Y **emen.** Unless the AK47 is added to the shooting at the Olympics it's unlikely any of us will ever hear the Yemen national anthem.

Z **imbabwe.** The thing about African dictators is that no one ever calls them on their bullshit -no one ever tells them the truth. We all have that one friend that keeps you in check - so when you try to roll up to the party dressed couture he'll be the first to remind you that you are not couture, in fact you are catalogue. But when you're an African dictator that doesn't happen. None of their boys are like, "Yo, Mugabe, bro. You're dressed like child pimp and not a pimp who sells children but a child who pimps. Is that a short sleeved suit!"? To be fair to the entourage of African dictators there's a higher than likely chance that voicing an opinion about their bosses clothing style could get them hung up on fish hooks by the Achilles tendons or genitally mutilated with the blade of a machete so I kind of get it, but because of this dishonest silence on their part, African dictators end up rolling around wearing some sky blue leisure suit nonsense when they could be wearing the skin of a leopard and fucking top hat! Mugabe looks like a little Jewish man from Florida who broke out the boot polish and went black face to bingo because his dementia has turned him into a vicious racist. Which, actually, in Mugabe's case isn't far from the truth.

You get to the point where it no longer matters what you do, wear, say or go to the toilet. That's a reward for having to hold it together for all the middle years and forcing yourself to be a fucking straight laced corporate nerd-hole and go to meetings when you should have been getting fucked up and jumping off a boat into the ocean. Old-age is shitty because you're dying fast and bits of you are shutting down and falling off of you and you're not cool any more but what you are is INVISIBLE and punish-proof. As long as you don't kill a motherfucker or fuck a kid you can pretty much do what you want. Telling people what you actually think of them alone is reason to get out of bed. Seriously- get on the MDMA, put some yellow speedos on and buy a flare gun and a megaphone and stop some traffic you hilarious old walking dead man. The world owes you some LULZ!

Age Gap. Men like to think the 'age gap' is when the gentleman is older than his perky breasted, ever-wet nubile new lover. But it's not. The 'age gap' is the space young people like to keep from sleazy old pricks with stray nostril hairs and breath that smell like regret, decay and menthol cigarettes.

Burden. Your refusal to gather on a cliff top en masse and step off on the rocks below exploding into a mush of grey hair and tissue thin skin is becoming a problem for the rest of us. This rapidly aging population is taxing our health services and making our public transport smell like corned beef. If you were as polite as you like to think you are, you'd all turn your pilot lights out on your heaters tonight and breathe deep.

Children. This is where kids finally show their worth. You wiped their arse and listened to their pointless, garbled, spitty-mouthed stories about a dog they saw. It's pay back time bitches. Wipe my old arse and guess what I saw today? I saw a fucking dog!

Dignity. As ladies get older their bladders start to go and their underwear starts to get wetter than a retards chin. As a husband, let me say that buying your tampons was one thing but when it comes to this leaky-lady shit you're on your own.

Everyone You Know Is Fucking Dead. Getting old is actually a nice way of saying 'getting alone'.

Fallen. If you have fallen and you can't get up it's time to consider staying down. You're halfway there anyway. Just start scratching and clawing a hole to roll into and just keep only breathing out. Getting up is one of the tenants of survival and not being able to get up is more than a clue it's time to assimilate with the worm shit.

Gum Jobs. Even with the arm skin that looks like an elephants eye-lid, the breath that smells like an extractor fan outside an abattoir, the penis that looks like a thalidomide's finger and needs 10,000mgs of Viagra to budge and the vagina that is as loose and floppy as Andre the Giants beanie-hat, geriatric sex is a thing. Which brings me to the idea of very, very, extremely assisted suicide.

Hands. Do what you want with your hat choices, face stretching and youthful wardrobe your hands will give you away as someone who once high-5'd Moses.

Invisible. Fact: When you become old aged you become invisible. This is one of the main thrusts for a mid-life crisis - wanting to be noticed. Congrats, bro *everyone* notices the 50-year-old at da club covered in 'running man' sweat who is now trying to explain the nuances of merlot to his new 19-year-old BFFs.

Just For Men. Try 'Clinging to it' Brown. Or 'I want it all back' black. Why not give 'Nothing more to live for' Auburn. They all look totally natural and manly and no one can tell even though it looks like you're wearing a home for lost cats on your fucked up old dome.

Keanu Reeves. There's a look that K-nu does when he's doing his 'acting'. He pulls it out basically any time he's supposed to think before he talks… You can nearly see his lips moving as he counts down from 5 before he speaks. It's that confused, concerned look. I guess he think it makes him look thoughtful - but it doesn't. He looks like

an old person. What it looks like is when you see an old person come into a room and completely forget whey they came into the room. That heady mix of confusion, terror and resignation that they're losing their minds and there's nothing they can do about it.

Lamborghini. None of us have a retirement plan because we live in the moment. And not in that freedom embracing 'carpe diem' way those Instagram inspirational quotes (digital herpes) tell us to do. You know the ones that show someone cartwheeling on beaches and spreading their arms out to the dawn and letting their vagina chakra shine. We all live in the moment; in that fingers in our ears yelling, "lalalalalalala" way. Like, "fuck it, I'll buy these new shoes even though I have 10 pairs just like them and let's go out for dinner on a Wednesday and drinks on a Thursday and keep buying and snorting coke until Sunday and I'M GONNA LIVE FOREVER kind of way. So when we get to retirement age it's going to be a rude, cat food filled, living in a tent on a traffic island, using a carpet as a blanket, awakening. You need to plan for your retirement so that doesn't happen. I have a plan. It involves a toe-nail-pink convertible Lamborghini (paid for by a high interest payday style loan I could find) a hand gun, a giant Irish wolf hound named Lexi, a heroin habit and a pair of bright yellow speedos. The plan is simple. I drive around in the Lambo nodding on heroin, wearing the yellow speedos and blasting the handgun into the sky. In the passenger seat sits Lexi with her head 3 feet above the roof of the car. Then when I get pulled over and the cops ask me if I have a license I say, "For the car, the dog or the gun?" and shoot the dog in the leg while I floor it. I'll either be shot by the cop, mauled by the dog or crash the Lambo into a tree - either way, who gives a shit I'll be high as Wilt Chamberlains dick. Golden years, indeed.

Monarchy. Let it go for fucksake. We live in democracies in the 21st century. If you want some old lady to wave at you from a window throw a rock at an old ladies window.

Nocturnal. Getting up every morning at 4am is basically like being a slightly late sleeping vampire.

Osteoporosis. I see old people in the street all hunched over looking like cashew nuts made of disap-pointment and I just want to grab them from behind and bear hug the old cunts and crack their spine all straight like CRRRRRAAAAC-CCKKKKKK-KKK-AKAKAKAAK-KK-KKKKKK and whisper "You're welcome!" in a low, low growl.

Pedophile. Even though you're not a pedophile you now look like you are a pedophile. Men over 55-years-old with kids on their laps or holding hands with a kid instantly looks fucking creepy. Now we understand that you're definitely NOT a pedophile (because getting it up takes ages and kids don't have the patience to wait that long) but, in the same way society doesn't want gay men teaching kindergarten (sorry Gays), we don't want old men playing horsey rides with our kids either.

Quest. The movie of your life is a comedy / suspense thriller. And it's just you walking around your house looking for your wallet, phone, keys, sunglasses, pen, phone again... Leaving the audience on the edge of their seat wondering if I'll ever leave the house this morning. It'll be called DUDE, WHERE'S MY EVERYTHING?

Racism. You might not have been racist during your youth but that liberal bull-shit is about to end. You may not even think you're being racist and might still think you have center left leanings but you'll start sentences with "I'm not a racist" or start calling black people 'chappies' then before you know it you won't take the change from the Indian shopkeepers hand and you'll blame the Jews for the banking thingee your saw on the whosamawhatsit.

Shady Brooks. Bring that retirement home shit on! I'm a fan of sitting in a chair and being spoon-fed ice cream with a TV that's on too loud. I like table tennis, golf carts and be-ing able to fart with im-punity because your whole world smells like cabbage anyway. That sounds good to me. Shit, I might roll up to a village now put on some sneakers with velcro on them, pull my pants up to my nipples and take a nap while driving a golf cart.

Too Fucking Late. Well. That was your life. There it went. I hope you didn't waste it living a lie or believing one. Try to set-tle in, make peace with your kids and start to prepare for death. What ever you do

don't, for fucksake, try to make up for lost time or believe those retirement commercials and think it's time to swim in a frozen lake, take up dancing or go to some place filled with native peoples. Now is not the time to start that novel or paint. No one thinks it's not too late for you to live with 'verve' and for the love of God don't rediscov-er your passion for life. You had your chance at all that shit but you decided to work and raise a family and be a productive member of society you fucking sap - now do what you did with all your dreams and hopes when you were young: squash them into a tiny ball and hide them deep inside yourself and just be glad you'll only have to live with the dis-appointment of a the failed experiment called your life for a couple more years.

Unbearable. Becoming an insufferable old prick is nature's way of making no one really give a shit-fuck-ing toss when you die. If you died the cool person you were in your twenties and thirties we'd all be distraught and affected by your passing but now you're an annoying old prick your passing is something we'll be over as soon as we leave the funeral - and about that. Who has funerals any-more? Just do a memorial page on Facebook and we'll all LIKE it or whatever. Fuck you're un-fucking-bare-able!

Values. Oh it's you! You're the one with the values these scoffing politicians keep banging on about and making terrible fucking decisions on behalf of. 'Family Values' have been dead since the Internet became available on our phones and 'Christian Values' is just code for 'I have guns'. Time for you to take your values, fold them up into ball the size of a piglets head and shove them up your slack old ass pipe.

Will. Why not just have a locked box with last will and testament stenciled on it and when you die have them open it in a room devoid of furniture with plastic sheeting on the floor. And when your kids and relatives ask, "What the plastic sheeting for?" your lawyer can say – "You'll see." And then unlock the box to reveal some polo mallets, one or two pick axe handles and a couple of blades and then get the lawyer to say. "Last man standing gets the lot… HUNGER GAMES, BITCHES!"

X (generation). If you remember MTV, Pulp Fiction, optimism, fossil fuel, education, white people's first fling with hip-hop, a gay friend, a black friend, smoking, home ownership, AIDS (that actually did it's job), bigger hair, dial up internet, landlines, jobs (where people actually built things), turning up for things you said you'd turn up to, people famous for achieving things, harmless McDonalds, harmless Coca-Cola, coolish Microsoft, cool Tom Cruise, FRIENDS, Seinfeld, Greenpeace, and littering. You have a virus called nostalgia and death is the best cure.

Yacht. Hey you, old dude all tanned and steely eyed on the bow of that 25-foot schooner popping Viagra and totally D.T.F. A man's penis is like one those original Disney films filled with Princesses, talking insects and sexists. It should be put in a drawer to gather dust it shouldn't be revamped and inflicted on the next generation.

PORNO GRAPHY

Two th.

Two things men: be honest and realize that part of what you're jerking off to is the degradation of women and the fact that this girl has made some pretty bad life choices to end up shovelling a black dick into her mouth that's so big it looks like a prosthetic leg dribbling a soccer ball and she's not having an unpainful time. And the other thing: notice how fast you slam the lid of your laptop after you've ejaculated. That's what I call 'at the speed of shame'. Porn is not the healthiest thing on the planet and it's making a generation of men who are addicted to easy orgasms. Men are getting used to the ease of it and that's one of the habit-forming traits. Men are addicted to chitchat free orgasms, and it's affecting their perception of how sex comes to them. Sex was never supposed to be easy to get. We were supposed to work for it. Sex is a powerful and wonderful dynamic because it is withheld. The sex dynamic twas ever thus: men want sex - women withhold it, and men become better people in order to get it. When a women holds out, a man stops acting like a moron and starts stringing sentences together and using the toilet like a big boy and this gets him his reward. The second World War was won by a bunch of virgins trying to make sure that the Germans didn't diddle their women.

Addiction. Every 39 minutes a new pornography video is being created in the United States. Every second 280,258 users are watching pornography on the Internet. Every second $3,075.64 is being spent on pornography on the internet. Every second 372 people are typing the word "adult" into search engines. 35% of all internet downloads are related to pornography. 25% of all search engine queries are related to pornography, or about 68 million search queries a day. Search engines get 116,000 queries every day related to child pornography. 2.5 billion emails sent or received every day contain porn

Brazilian. If you see a woman with pubic hair these days you think she's a lunatic. See a woman with natural, bushy pubes and you assume that she lives in the woods making Blair Witch twig sculptures and talking to sparrows.

Cunt. In porn everyone talks dirty. Talking dirty is an art and not something you can just do. The times I tried it I got way too into it and killed the mood. But that can happen when you stand on the edge of the bed and growl, "I want to watch your mother take a shit on the train!"

Dick dick dick dick dick dick dick dick. Thanks to porn the average heterosexual man in the year 2014 has seen as many dicks as a the average homosexual man in the year 1989.

Erectile Dysfunction. As more studies are done it's becoming apparent that one can have a healthy sex life or whack-it to porn. But not both.

Fathers. Without terrible fathers there would be no porn industry and us men would be back to being hunched over bra catalogues - so next time you hear about an absentee father missing his 8-year-old daughters birthday - give the guy a break… or try spanking it to a memory of a bikini mannequin.

Glory Hole. A hole in a wall where a dude pokes his dude through a hole in a wall and a someone on the other side of the wall sucks said dude. For heterosexual men it's a fantasy that only exists in porn. For homosexual men it's a Wednesday night.

Horse. This 'H' could also be 'Heroin' because you have to be a desperate, desperate, smack head to have sex with a horse.

...**I**.L.F. '...I'd Like to Fuck'. This equal opportunities acronym M.I.L.F, G.I.L.F, D.I.L.F made the industry billions by giving old people like your Mum, Granny and Dad jobs. Blow jobs.

Javelin Thrower's Arm. Ladies, look around you - most men have one arm notably bigger and stronger than the other arm and one hand with the grip strength of a pit bulls jaw and it's not because they represented their country in the Javelin.

Kim Kardashian. In 2007 Kim Kardashian made a porn tape. A year later her whole family gets a TV show and we have been getting gangbanged by them ever since.

Liars. There are two types of men in the world. Men who habitually use pornography and men who are liars.

Memory Wank. R.I.P memory wanks. I haven't had a memory wank since I was 15 years old and I'm not sure I could now. I'm so conditioned to only be able to whack it watching someone else demeaning themselves. If you trapped me on a desert Island I would have to hunt some monkeys down to watch them monkey-hump in order to get me going (is it doggy style if monkeys are doing it?).

Nymphomaniacs. When a woman wants to have sex all the time she's called a nymphomaniac. When a man wants to have sex all the time he's called Geoff or Darren or Mike...

Orgasm Envy. Have you seen the way pornstars have orgasms? The women could wake up Thor with their screams and the dudes could use the force of their ejaculate to control a race riot. Normal people's sound like the bored sigh of librarian and look like the stunted sneeze of a sparrow.

Photography. This is the sequence of events at the moment photography was discovered: "Hey look everyone I have invented a process whereby images of life can be captured on film and reproduc... NAKED WOMEN!"

QWERTY. Does any one know how to clean a laptop kkkkkkkkkkkkeyboard? For some reason my 'KKKKKKKKKKKK' kkkkkkkkkkkkkey kkkkkkkkkkk-kkkkkeeps getting stuckkkkk-kkkkkkkkkkkk.

Reality. Porn world and the real world are very different places because in the real world when you go to the launderette to do your laundry you go to the launderette to do your laundry.

Story Lines. There used to be storylines and plot in porn. Man delivers pizza to convent. And character development. Nun is revealed as cum-thirsty slut who ALSO loves pizza. But they were dropped for the easier to follow plot of 'they fuck'. It saved a lot of nervous set-up time in lounge rooms while wives were shopping and a lot of wear and tear on the fast forward mechanism in VHS machines.

Tiny Penis. I for one would like to see a genre of porn where men have tiny penises instead of these skin battering rams that take two hands to hold. Why? Umm... just... umm... because.

Uncle. In my teenage days porn wasn't as ubiquitous as it is now. In fact all available porn was stolen from one Uncle who owned a beer fridge with a babies urine sample in it, a motorcycle with a girls name and jeans so dirty and filled with microscopic life they came when called.

Virtual Reality. Oculus Rift, the VR headset maker, was recently bought by Facebook for $2bn because Mark Zuckerburg is sick of only jerking off to your holiday swimsuit photos at his desk.

Wacca-wacca-wow-wow. New word: 'Masturbatehoven' The person who composes the soundtracks for porn.

X-Rated. How quaint. X-rated seems like a simpler time. A time before gagging, DP, Red Rhapsody, Crying, Pegging, Fisting, Gape, Transman, Cuckold, Yiffy, Trampling... and everything the Japanese are doing.

Yellow Gold 22. Because the 21 other films of girls pissing on dudes *didn't quite* nail the idea.

Zillions. Just think of the countless millions of babies that never happened because they ended up in crumpled up tissues and dirty socks.

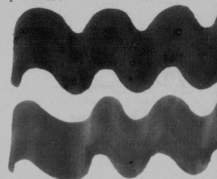

"THINGS WRITTEN IN QUOTATIONS ~~SEM~~ SEEM MORE PROFOUND THAN THEY REALLY ARE"

- Me Just Now.

Ask Not What Your Country Can Do For You... Ahh the good old days when you could stand up, muster a straight face and simply *guilt* people into sending their kids off to kill the innocent and die in the mud. Now you have to blow up a few of your own buildings and disappear a couple of airliners.

Be The Change You Want To See In The World. Why aren't any of the quotable folks more... average. It's all about making some big effort the whole time. Changing yourself or following your dreams. Why couldn't Gandhi have said, "Sit down, watch some telly, and eat some cake washed down with cold beer." I bet the skinny little cunt thought that thought all the time.

Cash Rules Everything Around Me. Ummm, move.

Dance like nobody's watching. Love like you've never be hurt. Sing like nobody listening. Say shit like this like nobody likes you.

Einstein. "Only two things are infinite, the universe and human stupidity, and I'm not sure about the former." Quoting smart people is a sure way to make yourself look... like you're quoting a smart person.

Fuck You, Dad! Jesus.

Give me a museum and I'll fill it - Pablo Picasso. Wow, Pablo. There are heavy weight boxers that aren't that cocky.

Historicalising History. "I know the human being and fish can coexist peacefully." George Bush "They misunderestimated me." George Bush "Families is where our nation finds hope, where wings take dream." George Bush "I just want you to know that, when we talk about war, we're really talking about peace." George Bush "I'll be long gone before some smart person ever figures out what happened inside this Oval Office." George Bush "There's an old saying in Tennessee -- I know it's in Texas, probably in Tennessee -- that says, fool me once, shame on --shame on you. Fool me -- you can't get fooled again." George Bush "Our enemies are innovative and resourceful, and so are we. They never stop thinking about new ways to harm our country and our people, and neither do we." George 'motherfucking' Bush.

I have a dream. The power of oration and well-chosen words. One stirring speech and America's race problem was solved... wait.

Jay Z. That's a crazy amount of problems for a rich guy, dude.

Kanye. While we're on rappers, Kanye should change his name to Quote-tron 2000. As one of the greatest comic creations of all time we need him on Earth. 'Kanye West' is actually a 20 year comedy project by Joaquin Phoenix and a host of expert effects practitioners from Hollywood. Have you ever seen Kanye West and Joaquin Phoenix in the same room? Exactly.

Lyrics. When someone comes to you with real world problems that require real world solutions but you can't be fucking arseholed helping the loser a great thing to do is just quote some song lyrics at the prick. So they might say, "I got my girlfriend pregnant and she wants to have an abortion but I'm not sure we should. I think I should maybe marry her?" And you say "You gotta know when to hold em. Know when to fold em." And then make your fingers into a phone shape, say "ring ring-ring ring… Sorry, I gotta take this." And leave the fucking room.

Martini. "Any man who is under 30, and is not a liberal, has no heart; and any man who is over 30, and is not a conservative, has no brains." The thing to remember about Churchill is that he was generally drunk. Which goes to cement his genius even further considering the only memorable thing the rest of us ever said when were drunk was shit like "Juzt the tip. Go on… I'll Juzt put in the tip."

"**N**o Shit" - Sherlock.

Oscar Wilde. "Some cause happiness wherever they go; others, whenever they go." Is not the same as "Shut up bitch. You're fat anywayz." But thanks to Oscar, now every gay dude with an unbusy mouth thinks they have the whole razor-sharp-cutting-wit thing sewn up as a birthright.

Post-it-notes. If your problems can be fixed by reading little affirmation notes you stuck on your mirror - you don't have fucking problems.

Quote Of The Day Calender. You poor poor poor poor poor poor poor poor poor poor poor poor poor poor poor poor poor poor poor poor poor poor poor poor poor poor poor poor poor poor poor poor poor poor poor poor poor poor poor poor poor poor poor poor poor poor poor poor poor poor poor poor poor poor poor poor poor poor poor poor poor poor poor desk bound cunt.

Repetitive Strain Injury. Spending more than 10 minutes on Instagram or Facebook could leave you at risk or RSI from rolling your fucking eyes so extremely and so often that cornea tears are a distinct possibility. Just looking at the cutesy little quotes set against sunsets, hand holding, love hearts in the sand and rain running down windows makes my pupils want to look at the dark blackness of the inside of my skull even if it means detaching them completely and ending up with cookie monster eyes that bob around independent of each other. BEAUTY BEGINS THE MOMENT YOU DECIDE TO BE YOURSELF. You fucking cunt. This digital herpes is the fault of some middle class women who lack any substance or fortitude and have zero real problems and rudimentary Photoshop skills. When they produce and post a quote like FALL SEVEN TIMES. STAND EIGHT. They aren't fighting real life adversity - they burnt their tongue on a Pumpkin Spiced latte. No matter what they say all those fucking quotes say the same thing I'M POSTING THIS QUOTE BECAUSE I WANT SOME ATTENTION AND IT'S EASIER TO POST THIS DROSS THAN TO HAVE AN ORIGINAL THOUGHT IN MY OWN CODDLED, SPOILT, LAME, BASIC-ASS HEAD.

Shit Happens. Like all wisdom, bumper sticker wisdom often comes to you right before you crash head first into something.

They. 'They' are some busy motherfuckers aren't they. They certainly say a lot of things don't they? I wonder if they get together once a year and think of a whole slew of shit to say so people like your mother can passively aggressively remind you not to / to do things without having to take responsibility for saying the thing themselves. They could be right though - you are a bit of a shambles.

Understated. God is Dead.

Viet Kong. "No Viet Kong ever called me nigger." The greatest of all time.

"**W**oah Wa Wee Wa" - Every fucking idiot for 12 months after that movie Borat came out.

X. "Sometimes you have to pick up the gun to put the gun down". When Malcolm was saying things like this they let him live and gave him a microphone. As soon as he returned from Mecca and started preaching that togetherness gospel - they picked up their guns.

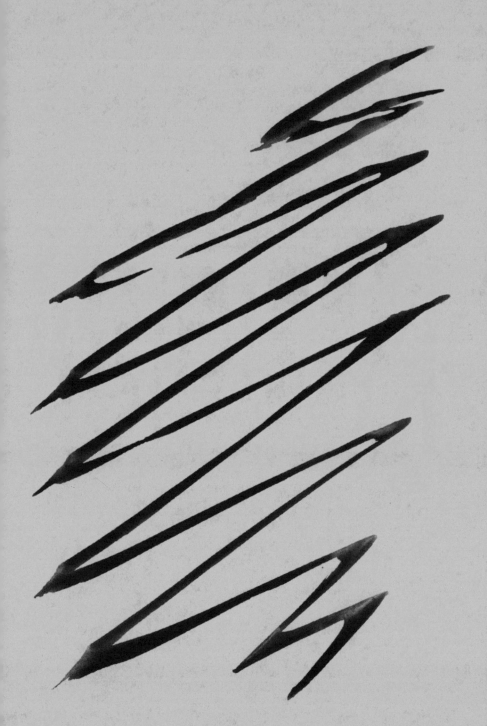

Easily the shittiest thing in the world.
Religion is a magnifying glass for the
worst traits humanity has. It attracts
the dumbest, least thoughtful and least
worthy among us and gives them a
golden megaphone, a lobotomy and
chequebook. It truly is like ~~handling~~
handing a chimp a handgun and a
Samurai sword and asking it to babysit.
If it were possible to cut this cancer
out of society and history we, as a
people, would be so much better off.
Fuck it and fuck you if you practice it.
All gods must be kept on a leash.

After Life. Religions are basically death cults that tell their followers that being dead is way better than being alive. A couple of questions: If I die old do I live as old for eternity? What if I die as a baby - do I stay a baby for eternity? Or can I choose to 'Frankenstein me' from my entire life - like a greatest hits of me? Can I spend eternity with a teenager's stiffy, a 20-year old face, a body before I got all these midlife crisis tattoos that make me look like a pad someone left next to a telephone, and maybe some 17-year old hands instead of mine which look like I'm wearing gloves made from Madonna's clitoris.

Beheading. Cutting peoples heads off is a PR move on the part of some of the more fringe Islamic groups. I can imagine the meeting with their PR agency now: "So guys, Janet had a really out of the box idea for getting some attention on social media. Our Janet is KRRRR-azy, she is. Anyway we were thinking you do some sort of speech to camera and then hack the heads off some Americans? Where do you get your ideas, Janet?!"

Celibacy. Priests have to swear a vow of celibacy because God needs his priests frustrated and maladjusted. But because priests are animals like the rest of us - not pure vessels of a nonexistent God's nonexistent love - priests do have sex, but they try and cover it from their God's view. Apparently God can't see priests have sex if they secretly hide their erect penises inside a child. Or maybe God has his hands over his eyes because it's so disgusting He just can't watch.

Door Knocking. Knock Knock. Who's there? Seventh Day Adventists. Seventh Day Adventists who. Seventh Day 'you're going to burn in hell for eternity because you are a moral-free pile of hot sin… can we come in for a cup of tea?' Adventists.

Evolution. "Are you seriously telling me that my great, great, great, great, great, great great, grandfather was a monkey?" Said no atheist ever.

Fundamentalist. At least you know where you stand with the hardcore zealots. It's the moderate modern 'pick n choose' Bible selectivist pussies that upset me the most. You either take it literally or you're not a believer. I'd rather have my hand cut off for stealing or be stoned to death for adultery than have to listen to some Christian rock band tell me how Jesus is "gonna rock my soul." You can't have it both ways Christian with the jeans tucked into his boots and crucifix round his neck that looks like the X game logo. Now go and put your wife in the shed, Jesus-boy – she's menstruating.

Grammys. The Grammys are a music award that Jesus has heavy involvement with. I think he might even have a hand in creating the thing. Maybe he's a financial backer or some sort of exec-producer? It's something important because every rap or country music artist that wins a Grammy says they couldn't have done it with out him.

Hell. This is the big reveal arena. Where the religious find out which faith was right after all. If you're a Jew, you die and feel the flames licking at your feet… It means you were wrong, your whole life was a waste of time and now you have to spend eternity in Hell. Maybe you'll be in Hell with the Catholics… Hey look Jewish film reviewer it's famous actor, director and catholic Mel Gibson… Awkward.

Indoctrination. The best time to get someone involved in religion is when they will believe anything you tell them. That's why kids are so valuable to religion. Santa brings you presents, the tooth fairy brings you money and some dude you don't know died all because of you and if you touch your penis you'll burn in hell for eternity. Night, night. I love you.

Jesus Mohamed Tom Cruise. When deciding on your religion it's important to understand your prophet because this is the guy you'll mostly be dealing with. God, Allah and L Ron are all upper management and don't do day-to-day stuff. The prophets are the business end of the deal. So: Jesus was an Arab, Jewish rebel who became a Zombie. Mohammed was an illiterate merchant's son who liked his chicks to look like Ninjas and Tom Cruise is a homosexual pantomime proponent who takes his teeth out every night and stores them in a nuclear powered whitening furnace… And they all want your money.

Kill, Thou shalt not... Religion lays claim to inventing morals. As physicist, Steven Weinburg said, "Religion is an insult to human dignity. With or without it you would have good people doing good things and evil people doing evil ... But for good people to do evil things, that takes religion."

Last Judgment. A staggering 44% of voting Americans (146 million people) believe that, within the next 50 years, Jesus will literally descend from heaven to judge the living and bring the faithful up to heaven. Far from being benign, these Christians Fundamentalists feel that concern for the environment and planet is futile. In fact they actually welcome the destruction of our environment, as it's a sign of the Apocalypse and when they get to sit on God's knee like a celestial mall-Santa. This wouldn't matter except they vote for people who share their views and create environmental policy. I reckon if Jesus turns up he's gonna be pissed because when he turns water into wine it's gonna taste like the Fukushima Nuclear leaks.

Mysterious Ways. God makes rainbows, baby pandas sneeze and poor Hispanic people win the lotto because God loves us and this is his proof. But when he sends a hurricane into a pediatric cancer ward, let's millions of people die of starvation, watches on while thousands are murdered in his name or makes some people ginger headed. It's not God hating us - that's impossible he's umm, just working in 'mysterious ways' we're just not meant to / riddled with tumors / nine-years-old to understand.

Nigerian AIDS Orphanage. The Catholic Church and 1.2 billion Catholic people think that condoms help the spread of AIDS and shouldn't be used. What do you think little Mataboombi? Mataboombi? Mataboombi can't answer because AIDS coma.

Omeisauras. A 20m long dinosaur that, according to religious people, could have made a great pet because they think the Flintstones was a documentary.

Psychiatric Wards. Mental hospitals everywhere are filled with people making the claims that the founders of the big three religions made. "I'm the son of God. I'm the messiah." All the 'messiahs' scream out while they paint symbols and diagrams on the walls with their own shit. Again, giving us all a valuable lesson in 'timing is everything'.

Richard Dawkins. This guy is the Atheist's Pope. Atheism is another faith based belief system except Atheists don't have faith that there is a God, they have faith that there isn't a God. Atheism is a bit like the other 'isms' except they don't have prayers, sermons Churches or Mosques they have dinner parties, Chardonnay and cheese plates.

Sin. Jesus died for your sins. So make his death worthwhile and sin the shit out of it!

Thought Crime. God being Omnipresent means that even your thoughts can be considered sins punishable by everlasting anguish. It's a totalitarian regime with a leader who wants to control your every action and your every thought. Which, I guess is why most religious people stop having them all together.

Underwear (magic). Mormons are a polygamous cult that hates vaginas. They think vaginas are literally the worst thing on the planet. So they try and destroy every vagina they meet by making their women stay pregnant and push as many little pussy wrecking fundamentalists out of them as possible.

Virgins. For Muslim Jihadists, heaven is basically a brothel filled with virgins. Question: Who wants to have awkward, tearful sex with virgins? I had sex with a virgin once when I was 16. It was harrowing. Her Mother found out and her father nearly beat me to death. Wouldn't it be better if heaven were filled with Glaswegian sluts? You might even get a finger up your arsehole while you were gobbed off.

Women. If you're a woman that likes being subservient, being treated like a second class citizen, having men tell you what you can and can't do with your own body, walking around under a sheet and generally shutting the fuck-up then you'll love religion.

Xenu. A science fiction writer named L Ron Hubbard invented a religion a few years ago. He called it Scientology. By his reckoning an intergalactic dictator named Xenu brought his people to earth 75 million years ago and killed them all with H bombs and now their souls have become Thetans which inhabit our bodies and cause us harm... People these days think it's crazy. Apparently claims of resurrection, talking bushes, turning water into wine, angels and the fact that the whole human race comes from two people is fine as long as it happened a really long time ago.

Yahwey is God's other name. He has this other name to check into hotels and because people say the word "God" way too often and it upsets his concentration when he's trying to map out and plan the lives of his followers and smite those who doubt. For example: people call "God" out during sex and Yahwey doesn't want to look down and catch your father in a wig getting pegged by your mother wearing a strap on they lovingly named "the persuader".

Zeus. There have been literally 1000's of Gods throughout history that people swore up and down were the one true God. Thor, Rangi, Amun, Odin, Tabaldak and Zeus to name but a fraction. That's why people should just calm down about this current batch. All it's gonna take is one dirty Nuke and Allah, Buddha and The Holy Trinity will be a distant memory and we'll all be worshipping 'ClickityClick The Cockroach King'.

A water cooler soap opera for men.
Gay by proxy. A pantomime of purpose.
Sport is superfluous and all at once
necessary. It's needed because it funnels
some of the pent up aggression and
uselessness out of men and helps us deal
with the fundamental truth that we
are lame. We need it because we
are all secretly gay, just some of us
have the balls to admit it - come on
'bro' you're walking round with another
mans name on your shirt - you're
either his property or you want to
paint water colours of him while he
towels off after a sauna.

"A hundred and 10 percent" What every athlete promises he'll give to win. That's because both the other team and basic mathematics are gonna get a beating out there on that field today.

Britain. The Motherland of all sport. Britain invented football for the Brazilians to beat them at, Rugby for the Kiwis to wallop them at and Cricket for the Aussies to give them a hiding at.

Commercial Breaks. Tiger Woods has learnt $1.1 billion from sponsors in his career. Nike, Titlest, Gillette, Accenture, Pepsi CO, EA Sports, but ironically his best advertising work was done for skanky Las Vegas strippers and hard faced prostitutes.

Dave. It must be annoying for sports stars to have their lives commentated on the whole fucking time. But you'll never know because you'll never know a sport star. The only way you'll ever know is to commentate someones life and see what happens... Start very early in the morning and don't stop until bedtime. Pretend you are a commentator and that your spouse, friend, travel companion or just some stranger you like the look of, is a sporting match that needs your analysis and insight. Constant analysis and insight. "Dave has woken up and oooh. He doesn't look pleased to see me in his bedroom. Looks like Dave has got a little morning friend in his trousers that he should cover up with a blanket." "Dave is eating his lunch with a look on his face that could be anger or could be frustration and now – oh no! Dave has lost his temper and he's lashing out with a chicken bone and fork. There is chicken everywhere and Dave is showing the speed he's famous for as he chases me out of the restaurant, into the street." "Dave is rocking and hugging his knees. It's been a long day and I'm sure Dave would like to sleep now. Maybe we can get a quick interview. Dave you look upset. Are you okay mentally or close to snapping for good?"

ESPN. Sport is really just a gigantic, high-priced soap opera so men have something to talk about and don't have to stare awkwardly at each other at social occasions.

FIFA. If you're interested in hosting a soccer world cup in your country, FIFA are the people you bribe to make sure that happens FYI: It might cost you a little more if you plan to fragrantly abuse human rights, displace families or enslave workers in the production of your stadiums but for 2 weeks your hotels, bars and prostitutes will be full.

Golf. Being good at golf is just admitting you no can longer stand your wife but you're too cheap to get a divorce.

Hooligans. While fans of most sports are making plans to meet up in a bar and have a couple of beers after the game, football fans are making plans to meet up in some abandoned cement works and attack each other with hammers and box cutters. Or maybe hook up on the high street and chant some racist slogans and set fire to some immigrant businesses. Football players might be the biggest soft-cocks to wear a uniform but their fans are some of the scariest neo-Nazi hate criminals on the planet.

Idiocy. Idiocy is rife in sports with both fans and players being some of the biggest morons on the planet. It's not a bad thing. In fact it's vital. One needs to be idiotic to appreciate sports for what it is and not think about it too much. Thinking about men running after a ball wearing arbitrary colours in tribal surrogates with millions upon millions of people pas-

sionately caring about the outcome can lead to an existential rabbit hole where one finds oneself hopelessly lost just repeating the word "ball" to ones self and wondering what the point of any of the things we do in life are. Seriously? Ba-ll. B-a-ll. Baaaallllll.

Just Do It. Is what they yell at the people in the Chinese factories when their fingers are too cramped to thread laces on the fashionable running shoes anymore.

Ko. Mike Tyson once said, "Everyone has a strategy until I punch them in the face." He said other things too but his mouth was full of someone's ear so they came out all garbled.

Left Hook. Domestic violence rates go up after most big sporting matches. Some guy's team loses a game and his wife loses teeth because, as the saying goes, "If we lose the game on the field - we win the fight in the kitchen."

MMA. "Snap, tap or nap." Meaning you either break a bone, surrender or get knocked-the-fuck-out. If it wasn't for the fact people have to buy a ticket to see this crazy shit, anyone doing it would all be in a jail within a jail for assault.

Negro League. It used to be in America there were sports leagues for blacks and for whites. They were segregated by colour. Now there's only one league and it's still segregated. But this time by athletic ability.

Olympics. Every four years we get to drape ourselves in a flag and fight a proxy war sponsored by Coke. It's all so passive aggressive. They should just be done with all the 'spirit of the games' bullshit and make the Olympics the settling ground for any and all beef countries have had with each other over the past four years. It would mean combining the Javelin with the marathon, Archery with Gymnastics and boxing with swimming but fuck it let a few jocks sink to the bottom of a pool with a broken jaw - the medal ceremonies are too long anyway.

Parlour Games. Any game where the players can drink heavily and still compete is not a fucking sport. I'm looking at you darts, snooker and boxing.

Quiditch. Not only do nerds not play real sport they don't even read about real sport.

Referee. Remember that fat kid you used to push over, go to his house and steal his LEGO tell him that you fucked his mother, ate the yogurt from his school lunch for a year and picked last anytime you played sport? Well he got himself a whistle and a fetching black and white shirt and now he wants revenge.

$ons. With sports stars salaries being in the stratosphere, if you have a son you have a potential goldmine on your hands... All it takes is total mind control and domination from the moment they're born - also if you're a skinny, weak Caucasian dude you might want to plan an African safari and come back with a 'souvenir' inside your new wife that can dunk a basketball.

Team Building. There are many ways to foster a team spirit but nothing, it seems, beats taking turns on a passed out college student in a Holiday Inn after an away game.

Urine Test. There should be two lots of athletic competition. One for the athletes who are happy with the limits imposed by their human bodies and then the other for the athletes who want to use every possible advantage the human mind can conjure and put on a real fucking show! I'd love to see someone run 100m in 5 seconds and then see their heart explode like a piñata at a retarded kids birthday party. Or watch a guy snatch 1000kgs over his head and then go and punch a pensioner to death in an uncontrollable rage. What about a Judo match where limbs were torn off and then used as clubbing implements in those weird contactless Taekwondo matches? Let's get Russin about being fast, strong or violent for fucksake.

Volley Ball. Nobody watches women's sport. This is for two reasons. The first is that it's just a shitter, slower, more uncoordinated version of men's sport and the second is because men are sports fans not women and male sports fans don't really like watching women who are better at sport than they are.

WAG. A WAG is the wife or girlfriend of a sports star. The key to being a successful WAG is to master 'forgiving and forgetting' so when your shine starts to dull and the inevitable mistress / affair /rape allegation / scandal surfaces you can just go and get tested for stray STD's at the team clinic and head to the

"I'd like to apologise to my fans" press conference where you can smile like a waxwork and think of the jewelry you'll be adding to the stash in your hidden safe.

X-Mas Stocking. Every year the booksellers shelves groan under the weight of some sports star's 'biographies'. They mostly go like this. I was born. I played tennis. I won tennis. Tennis. Tennis? Tennis. And then I turned 22.

Yo-Yo. Is it racist to accept that black people are better at every single sport that white people invented? If white people want to win at some sports that aren't swimming or equestrians in the next decade may I suggest we start taking the yo-yo seriously and start looking for sponsors?

Zambroni. They say boxing is the most pure sport there is. The sweet science. In a way they're right. If you let any game carry on long enough it eventually reduces itself boxing. In the old days before sport got all faggy and athletes became breakfast cereal salesmen, fighting was a part of every sport - hockey got so bad they had to invent a ride on mower style machine and pull it out at halftime to mop up all teeth, blood and clumps of hair that would clutter up the ice.

The poorer and more hopeless you are the bigger your TV is. You can tell a working class family that's only a pay cheque away from not eating that week because their TV is a 92 inch monster that takes up half their hovel and everything it's possible to sit ~~sit~~ or lie down on is aimed at it. It's no accident that the more downwardly mobile you are the stronger your relationship with TV. This is not to mistake TV shows with TV. There are some stellar pieces of culture available to watch out there as any middle class cunt with a remote control will happily tell you over some cheese - but I'm talking about TV. Like, when you turn it on and watch it - TV. Do that and tether yourself to a downward spiral so dark and fast that the only good thing about it is that you'll black out and come to three years later owning a couch with a lever you can pull that makes a foot rest pop up. TV is hour after hour of people selling junk they found in their attic, teenagers ~~dr~~ drinking cocktails and texting each other, some other people training their dogs and then after that some rich cunts spending what you're going to spend on your child's education ~~money~~ on some clothes... for their child. Kill your TV before it kills you.

Another One? The box set has become middle class crack. If you're not a sleep deprived wreck who knows what "dookie got popped by the vacants" means or have a cursory knowledge of how to run a drug business from your living room you'll never win at dinner parties.

Black Screen. Did you know that all TVs come with an OFF button? It's actually the same as the ON button you just press it a second time and the TV switches OFF… And plunges your life into a silence so black and all encompassing that you can finally hear yourself thinking… Switch it back on! Switch it back on!

Cops. The original and best reality show. Police busting scumbag trash for our viewing entertainment. Which, if given a long enough timeline all reality shows eventually become.

Dads Chair. Ever flop into Dad's chair and squash out some air from the cushion? That's the smell of disappointed, male resignation. A million hot damp farts, drunk sleep sweat, snot wiping's and a kilo or two of rotting skin flakes all topped off with some spilt beer, gravy and a splash of late night wank-water that missed the fabric of Dad's track suit pants. No matter what your journey in life, it's this chair where you too will end up sitting through your whole second half.

Empathy. Something happens to you when you're shown a constant cycle of the world's problems on 24 hour News Channels. Something happens to you when you see the starving, war afflicted, lost and beaten down members of society peering out at you from behind a screen… unfortunately that something is 'nothing'.

Fifteen Minutes. Now we have DVRs and can fast forward TV, your fifteen minutes of fame has just turned into about 1 minute 30 seconds.

Gastroenteritis. As soon as someone invents a remote control that orders pizza the circle will be complete.

Here's One I Prepared Earlier. Women microwave terrible food and watch sumptuous cooking shows with amazing chefs the same way men jerk off onto their own stomachs and watch energetic threesomes with hot as hell porn stars. (see Dad's Chair).

Insomnia. If you're watching TV and wondering why you don't have a flat stomach and are starting to think that the wraparound electronic gut-melta might be the answer. If you're unemployed and watching some 11am telly and starting to think that maybe you could rock rock rock your way to better eyesight with the rocking cataract remover. Or if you have been missing out on nutrients in your water because you haven't been able to hold your urine in long enough and haven't got new urethra plugs... then you need to go volunteer at a soup kitchen or read a fucking book.

Jerry! Jerry! Jerry! Because dog fighting is still illegal and we actually care about the well being of dogs we use poor people instead. So rather than watching some dogs hurt each other, which would be heartbreaking, we just chuck some poor people on a badly designed set and let them hammer at it. Their women are always pregnant and seldom know whose dick was used to cause the baby, they often have missing teeth, wear sportswear even though they are fat, more than not have sex with family members AND when you put them on your TV show they fight each other so often the cameramen need to carry stun guns. It's basically wrestling without the eloquent oration.

Ka-chissssssssskkk. How good is that noise at the start of anything by HBO? It means what's about to happen is orgy of awesome and you're about to get bukake'd by brilliance.

Life Lessons. Thanks to TV I've been through war, adopted two black kids, been down... but not out, remembered who my friends were even though I got rich, had amnesia, like, 22 times, made some truly regrettable decisions on my wedding day, cut the red wire, jumped a shark, tasted the sweetness of the dish called revenge and been the man everyone knew I could be. What a life I've nearly lead.

Monkey See Monkey. Do Have you seen people being interviewed in the street lately? It's like everyone's on the red carpet. They all speak in sound bites. I'm not talking about the celebrity nit-wits with media training. I'm talking about some no-name father of three being asked what he's doing to prepare for the upcoming flood season. Watch him! He smiles broadly, looks directly to camera and says something salt of the earthy and folksy like, "Friend,

I'm from Aroobra - the only water that worries me is the water my wife tries to put in my whiskey." And then just drives away like a fucking boss.

News Corp. Yes Rupert Murdoch has an agenda. Yes he controls much of the information that washes over us. But maybe his greatest trick was to make news comfortable. To turn news into light entertainment. News was never supposed to be comfortable and it was never supposed to be entertainment. The job of News was to tell us hard to swallow facts about the world and our place in it. It was supposed to be adversarial, challenge the powers that be and challenge us and our own lazy conceptions and ideas. It was supposed to be the truth. But thanks to subscription based news channels, that singular, uncompromising goal of 'truth' has been replaced with a catalogue of 'truths'. Whatever your beliefs and assertions about the world - there's a news channel serving up that self same bullshit in a package that has the mechanism of fact, looks suspiciously like news but isn't the news. It's on in the background gently letting us believe what we want to believe, letting us feel comfortable.

Opium. 'They' don't need to have surveillance on every citizen all the time to know what they're up to. That's the one thing Orwell got wrong- they just need to film a bunch of rich housewives shrieking at each other through a haze of pain pills and white wine and put it on TV every night and they'll know exactly what 99% of us are doing. It don't watch us - we watch it.

Pester Power. When your 4-year-old kid walks up to you and says. "Mumma I want a Power Trooper, some captain Yum cereal and a Teddy Loves You or I'll kill myself" - that's called pester power and it's what happens when people let TV raise your kids.

Quiz Show. Remember the days before the Internet pushed it's heightened reality into our frail human frames and evicted our souls? Things were simple. The tough questions weren't posed by men in deserts while they cut the heads off aid workers. They were posed by 50-year-old men with perma-tans and lovely assistants and the answer were always just a commercial break away.

Remote Control. Before the remote control was invented people turned on their TV' like animals by walking over to it and touching a button that made a CLICK noise!!! What the actual fuck!!! Then they just had to choose ONE channel and watch that one channel like some sort of Neanderthal with an attention span. But now thanks to the remote we can and watch 20 seconds of 100 channels and treat our medulla oblongata like a the prettiest teenaged boy in an adult penitentiary.

Seinfeld. The TV only show that was *officially* about nothing.

Teleprompter. Live TV is the best because "George Bush doesn't care about black people."

Unplugged. How can you tell if someone you meet doesn't own a television set? Give them five minutes and they'll tell you.

Virgin-i-TV. How long until the number one show on TV is a 16-year-old girl with 20 men in their 40's competing to win the chance to pop her cherry? "Dennis is a 45 year old divorced father of three who recently took up kite surfing and lives in a studio apartment above a kebab shop. He wants to POP THAT CHERRY and is doing the danger run blindfolded for the chance of doing it without a condom." Oh yeah, that's what the show is called – POP THAT CHERRY and, depending on your religion and how many daughters you have, you can play a long at home.

Weeknights. Monday night to Thursday night you might as well just put your self into cryogenic freezing or just asphyxiate yourself with some carbon monoxide. You have no money, booze is off limits because your hangovers take two full days to recover from and you can't have sex without being drunk… So because you can't just seep into an induced coma without the risk of fucking up the dosage on the sleeping pill exhaust fume combo, here are some minor celebrities dancing competitively to kill your time. See you on Friday.

X-Factor. Recently a group of British kids were asked what they wanted to be when they grew up and their answer? "Famous". That's not just deluded and hilarious. It's nuts. They didn't even say a singer or an actor. They want to go round all that work bullshit and get straight to the fame part. They just want their whole lives to be one long karaoke. Where someone feeds them the work and they just stand there taking credit for it. Say what you want about kiddie porn but at least the kids suffer for their art.

Yelling. Men are now no longer hunter gatherers in a tribe of about 50 -70 people where their lives used to consist of hanging out with their mates solving problems, killing majestic game, BBQing, building shelters, fucking braided lovelies in the style of dogs and eventually dying in a glorious explosion of violence at the hands of rival tribes before heading to a mythical paradise to do the same shit all over again with ancestors and ultra baddass GODS! Now we are basically powerless, limp proxys of that and all our tribal instincts are funnelled into getting a beer buzz, watching sport happen on TV and yelling a bit… until we're told to shush by unbraided unlovlies. Go Chiefs!

Zone Out. Television sets have what's called a flicker rate. This flicker rate helps to switch off your critical functions and put you into a hypnotic state. This state is so addictive that I'm surprised you're actually reading the words on this page mainly because I'm surprised they're actually written.

-U-

UNIVERSE

Let's just keep it simple. And talk about the observable shit. Our sun is a million times more massive than the Earth. Our galaxy has a million million suns. The universe has roughly a million million galaxies. Not to mention all the planets and asteroids, comets, meteors and toaster ovens that live in each one of those galaxies - that is a lot of stuff and all of that stuff came from a point the size of a ~~proton~~ proton and no one really has a clue how and we sure as shit don't know why and maybe we never will. But the great thing about the Universe is that you only have to look at images from the Hubble telescope and see the vastness to remind yourself that you yourself are small as a proton and your credit card debt only really exists in the quantum world.

Anthropomorphic Principle. If a tree falls in the forest and no one is there to see it did the tree fall? If the Universe wasn't geared towards making us sentient would the Universe even exist? The Anthropomorphic Principle is human self-importance running wild. It states that the Universe is the way that is (the age and physical laws and properties) to support human life. This seems to ignore the natural selection process which is a painful journey of death, destruction and 99% extinction that we as a species have enjoyed and also seems to forget the FUCKING HUGE-NESS of the Universe and therefore the likelihood that life isn't anomalous and the exception but is probably the norm just because we can't find it, don't mean it aint there. And to answer that first question once and for all —If a tree falls in the forest and no is there to see it did the tree fall what do I need to say to stop you talking to me, hippy?

Big Bang Theory. There are two Big Bang Theories.
1: In less than 0.000000000 0000000000000000000000000 0.1 seconds, from something smaller than an atom came the known universe.

2. From something as dull than a room full of Jewish writer's imaginations came a sit-com.
The big bang is science's version of saying "Let there be light". It makes sense and all but the real juice is what happened before the big bang. Which, in theory one we still have no idea about. We know what happens in theory two: the Jewish writers drink a diet coke and put their New Balance clad feet on the writers table and say, "Okay guys, lets make another blight on our culture." But theory one might as well have been "God said, Abracadabra!"

Causality. Then someone yells out, "Yeah, mother-fucker but who made God?"

Dorks. When you say, "I had this interesting idea today." What you mean is you're going to make a frieze for your apartment out of some broken plates glued to wall. When the heroes of physics say "I had this interesting idea to-day." They mean they may have cracked quantum gravity and come up with a unified theory of everything and disproved the concept of God. Now who's the dork, Mrs. Gluegun?

Einstein. Einstein is probably the biggest genius to ever be born. In one year he published three game changing papers that are the foundation of modern physics and the way we understand the universe. But without a doubt his greatest gift to humanity was his gift to the feckless hacks in advertising. He invented the shorthand for 'brainiac'. If you're working in advertising and you're lazy (you work in advertising) a really good way to make your product look smart is to have a picture of Albert Einstein holding it, sitting in it, wearing it on his head, sucking on it, drinking from it, writing with it or lubing it up. Everyone from Apple to Pepsi have used the image of Einstein to tell dumb people that their product will make them smarter and for the most part it fuckin' works - because, lets face it, none of the rest us is Einstein.

Fourteen Billion Years. The Universe is bogglingly old. It's hard for our primate brain to truly understand the scale of the time the Universe has been around... without metaphors at least. So... If the Universe was roll of toilet paper (400 sheet is the average roll) the start of the Universe started when someone put it on the roll holder - but like the beginning of actual Universe no one knows how it happened - it just happened and maybe we'll never know how or who. Then for your first 4-5 poos there was just a hot plasma fog - which also now describes the state of your toilet - thick enough to taste and hot enough to make your eyes water (you ever do a poo that is so bad you take your tee-shirt off and throw it out of the room because you know that smell will infiltrate the fabric of your clothes like if you were smoking meth in a car?) and make some atoms and gases. Basically a Universe haunted with poo ghosts. From 5-7 poos, matter started to form - again look at your toilet now that's the matter forming on the walls of the toilet walls waiting for you to piss them off, and because we're all decent human beings and fold not bunch the toilet roll looks pretty much the same. Then from 7-15 toilet-times thanks to gravity, stars start forming. Nuclear reactors with the heat and ferocity of a pink sphincter licked with the brown tongue of a vindaloo shit. Then more gravity at about the 20-poo mark and the formation of galaxies and we're not even nearly halfway through the roll. Then at 8.7bil-lon years the formation of our solar system which is like running into the toilet and grabbing a few bits of TP because you just farted wetly and you want to under-stand if your arsehole still does it's primary role of stopping shit fall out. The Earth was formed at around 4 billion years or about 30 poos in and there's still some paper left on the roll but not much. You're start-ing to think about changing the roll… however one does that?! Let's fast forward and get past the dinosaurs and the fluke collision of an asteroid that ended their reign and then the rise of the mammals from rat like creatures to the human life you now are that is star-ing empty roll that winks back at you from the back of the cistern while you shuf-fle into the kitchen with a shitty arse and your pants round your ankles looking for some handy towel.

Gravity.

There's the grav-ity that makes fat people fall off horses and land in hilariously broken ways in videos on the Internet and there's the gravity that bends time in bamboozling ways. It's the same gravi-ty but one makes time slow down around huge objects and one makes time speed up when you're watching YouTube at work.

Hubble.

Edwin Hubble was the man who discovered that the stars and galaxies are moving away from each other and therefore the Universe had a beginning. Until that point scientists believed that Universe had always existed which was the only time in history that the religious clowns had one up on science because at least they had someone turning on a celestial light switch.

Infinity.

Some humans like to try and imagine a really really really really re-ally really really lot of something like sand in the desert but that aint in-finity. Some humans imagine heaven is infinite but then they talk about it being a place like an amusement park with a gate at the front so they'll never get it. Some humans like to make them-selves feel better by say-ing, "The fact that we are even contemplating infinity is amazing." That's a bit like telling a retard you're proud of him for not bit-ing the bus driver even when the retard travels to school on a tricycle. Infinity is not how much you love your kitten or a way to describe your 'potential' your mother uses. Infinity is what comes out in equations when the-oretical physicists haven't cracked it. It's deemed a flaw and makes them want to leap into the infinite gravity of a singularity... even though it shouldn't exist.

Large Hardon Collider.
The biggest experiment ever conducted and the largest microscope ever constructed... Who gives a fuck if they discover new particles or understand the conditions of the Universe at the Big Bang? The thing itself is enough. The largest machine ever constructed, it gets 100,000 times hotter than the centre of the Sun for fucksake. It's 27.5 km around firing a proton around the circuit just below the speed of light the proton will travel the giant circuit a staggering 11,245 times a second. The magnets in the machine produce more gravity that the earth by a staggering 100,000 times. And its major discovery is a parallel Universe where nerds are rock stars. Yeah there's particles getting smashed but there's also a shit ton of unkempt pussy getting bashed pretty hard too.

Microwave Background Radiation.
In 1963 two guys were tooling around with some faint microwave signals that were bouncing around our Milky Way and they discovered the earliest possible snapshot of our Universe

when the Universe was a mere 38,000 years old. And the snapshots of your kids are nice too.

Nobel Prize.
As opposed to the Nobel Peace Prize, which they just hand out these days even if you're responsible for more drone murders than any other President, the Nobel Prize for Physics is actually quite a tricky bastard to win. You have to have done things like measured the conditions at the moment of the start of the Universe, split the atom or discover dark energy. You know, shit that actually happened. It's a shame that these guys aren't more famous and well known. Holding these men and women in the proper esteem they deserve would be a step in the right direction for this backward rat nest of vain twits and cunts. We don't televise the Nobel Prize in Physics Awards because we're too busy giving awards to actors who pretend to be the people who win Nobel Prizes in Physics.

Observable.
There are the theoretical physicists and there are experimental physicists. One lot are concerned with what can be seen and measured and the other lot are the ones concerned with everything else. To over simplify the relationship, the theoretical rock

stars postulate things like black holes and the nerds come behind them with calculators and do the clean up. If this were a movie the theory dudes would be playing hacky sack and inventing crazy bongs and seeing the whole world with an animation overlay of graphs and tumbling numbers and the other experimental cats would be the Asian chick who wears glasses and has terrible fashion sense who reveals herself as integral in the battle against their common enemy - the jocks. And who we'll discover in the final showdown is sexy when she takes her glasses off and wears her slutty sisters red dress and pastel coloured heels and maybe some heavy blue eyeliner and… wait what where we talking about?

Quantum Mechanics.
So the particles that make up matter are in more than one place at once and it's not until we look at the particle that the particle settles on being in the place we look. So then our consciousness creates matter. Which means maybe those fucking hippes and self help turd smokers are right and maybe we all better start making a 'dream collage' and being 'nice' to people. My matter wants to be in another place.

Relativity.
If you got into a space ship and travelled near the speed of light you'd age more slowly than the rest of us left here on earth. Forget how, that fact alone should be enough for the richest Americans to pool their money with L'Oreal and get that age defying, light speed travelling space craft into launch mode as soon as yesterday.

Stringed Along.
When you get really small everything gets really weird. At the smallest levels of the universe might be vibrating strings. The strings that might exist might vibrate at different frequencies and create the observable Universe but also operate in different unseen dimensions to the standard three that we plod around in. They're also responsible for Wikipedia pages that are 22 meters long and word salads that aren't nutritious in the slightest.

Time.
Figure this out: Did time begin at the inception of the universe or is time eternal. IE is time linked to space or apart from space? Have a think and get back to me. I'll time you.

Uranus. A planet so named to keep school boys interested in astronomy.

Vacuum. When you're in a 'happy' marriage its about 4% talking about things that interest either of you, 22% talking about admin 72% heavy threatening fear filled, dreadful icy bitter silence - nothing. This is how marriages work. That dark, empty silence is the energy that pushes the marriage along - it's a fear of this encompassing vacuum overtaking the entire marriage that forces the married couple to come together and form things like dinner dates, shared jokes, and genital remembrance sessions (matter). This is a ratio we see in the empty cosmos too. About 4% matter, 24% dark matter and 74% dark energy. The 4% is the matter -the galaxies, stars... trips to Ikea, second hand SUV's, economy class boarding passes, celebrity chef cook books, empty wine bottles and all the other stuff you think is your marriage but it aint - it's the foreboding fear and dread that keeps it all together - it's the vacuum.

WTF. Seriously, Universe. What the fuck?

X= Understanding the Universe. If You really want to understand the universe it will require understanding mathematics. Mathematics is not necessarily the end game it was made out to be in . school. Mathematics is simply the language that's spoken when the brightest minds on our planet talk about and try to describe their ideas about the cosmos. Equally there's no point in being great at maths of you're not talking about the cosmos. Just being good at mathematics and not applying it to physics and astrophysics is like playing scrabble in Mandarin with the keynote speaker at the American Institute For American Speaking And Knowledge Avoidance Seminar... pointless.

You-insignificant-nothing. Look around you. You are a miracle of nothing. Take a deep breath, be grateful there's actually anything here at all and just try not to fuck the ride up for anyone else.

Zodiac Sign. Gemini:
You're a fucking gullible,
childlike idiot. Sagittari-
us: You're a fucking gullible
childlike idiot. Capricorn:
You're a fucking gullible
childlike idiot. Pisces:
You're a fucking gullible
childlike idiot. Virgo:
You're a fucking gullible
childlike idiot. Taurus:
You're a fucking gullible
childlike idiot. Scorpio:
You're a fucking gullible
childlike idiot. Leo: You're
a fucking gullible child-
like idiot. Cancer: You're
a fucking gullible childlike
idiot. Aquarius: You're a
fucking gullible childlike
idiot. Libra: You're a fucking gullible childlike idiot.
Aries: You're a fucking gullible childlike idiot. Stars
are gigantic nuclear reactors
not crystal balls you toddler
brained tool. The Universe
doesn't care about you and
you next job / love life /
run-in with a stranger baring
good news - the only thing
that astrology predicts accu-
rately is that if you believe
that fucking nonsense you're
about a third as bright as
someone who doesn't. And because of that intensely lazy
stupidity you're destined
for average, average, average
things.

VI
CE

Drugs are better than life. No one is honest about that. Doing drugs is better than just being alive without doing drugs. You want evidence? Fuck off and take some drugs. Here's the thing. If you're in your 20's and don't do drugs you've got no soul but if you're in your 40's and still do drugs you've got no brain. At some ~~point~~ point the drugs have to be left on the coffee table for the next generation and you have to leave the party - and the best way to leave a party is to do one massive line and race home in a cab and try and have sex until you pass out. Don't be a wrinkled old ~~scum~~ scum bag they have to push out the door on a wheelie stretcher. There's only one Keith Richards and you're just a couple of guys named Keith and Richard.

ATM. How do you know if you have a drug problem? If you're paying for drugs with crisp, new notes directly from an ATM you're probably okay. If you're paying for drugs with some crumpled up notes and some scraped together coins... it's touch and go. If the ATM you're using is your Mother's purse, kid's college fund, petty cash box from work, money from the wallet of man you just made unconscious with a bat, or your mouth, vagina or anus then seek some help.

Boredom. Drugs kill boredom as effectively as they kill ambition. It's not even a close contest. Drugs not only kill idle boredom they can also beat things that are actually boring. Take LSD and put your head in a paper bag. You could happily sit there for over an hour with that bag on your head completely unbored where as without drugs if I told you to get a paper bag you'd be bored before I finished the senten... never mind. Go look at your phone.

Coke Cock. Cocaine will make you as horny as a teenaged wolf and then, because it's an arsehole of a drug, make your cock look like the last letter 'I' in a bowl of alphabet noodles.

Dancing. Without drugs dancing would either be the type with a narrative or the type with sequins and both are inexcusable. The only good dancing is the self-assured, meaningful, flailing and face pulling that comes from being gills deep in as many different compounds as will fit into the little baggies hidden in your sweaty socks.

Exhaustion. Sometimes celebrities have to go to rehab because they're 'exhausted'. The celebrity isn't technically lying because staying awake for 4 days straight smoking pain pills, meth and shelving rocks of coke while paying prostitutes to squirt Moet laced urine on your chest does tend to take it out of you.

Fun. Sex is fun, music is fun, sunshine is fun, riding a skateboard is fun, friends are fun. But all those things are way more fun with drugs.

Gurning. "No officer I'm not on drugs, I just swallowed a matchbox full of fleas."

Hugs. These were supposed to be some magic thing to replace drugs. Hugs not drugs was the catch phrase. But it never took off be-

cause hugs are wildly in-
ferior to heroin - we know
that because no one ever
sucked a dick, murdered a
parent or shot a cop in the
face for a hug.

I ntervention. There's
something about watching a
TV program about addicts
being forced to quit drugs
that makes me want to get
high as a giraffes nuts.

J unkie. If you're read-
ing this you're not a junk-
ie. Junkies don't read books
they sell them next to some
stolen DVDs, a watch that
doesn't work, a laptop box
and three random remote
controls on a stretched out
blanket outside a 7/11.

K . Somewhere there's a
horse who can't get that
operation it needs because
some pasty faced teenager
is sitting on a couch in a
rave feeling like he's in
the bottom of a well, his
hands are a kilometer away,
he can't close his mouth and
saliva is falling out of it
like a popped water balloon
and he's having the best
night of his young life.

L esbianism. The things you
do sexwise when you're on
drugs only count 30%. So if
you're normally a straight
woman but you take drugs and
end up with your face in a
pussy bobbing for clits it's

fine. You can still wake up
and be a vanilla breeder.
And if you fuck someone you
just met that's also fine.
Even dudes. If you're a
dude that usually only fucks
chicks but your fuck a dude
without a condom while you
scream out, "I'm Mommies big
boy and I'm taking what's
mine!" That's also fine.
Tomorrow after you wash your
dick just say, "Pffft I was
on drugs." And go to that
darling little brunch spot -
straight-guy style.

M iami Vice. The war on
drugs costs the US government around $ 51 billion a
year and yet I can get a guy
to drop off a gram of cocaine
to my house in less than 30
minutes for 50.00 bucks. On
a Monday… at 4am. Nice work
Tubbs and Crockett you linen
wearing, pastel pooftas.

N aloxone. Heroin is quite
the 'distracting' drug. It's
been known to 'distract'
people from their jobs,
families and whole decades.
Sometimes heroin users need
help getting undistracted
and that's where Naloxone
comes in - it's an opiate
blocker that renders the
effects of heroin null and
lets users come back to being a tax paying member of
society where they can be
distracted by sport, celebrity, a SALE on pants and
pictures of baby otters on
their newsfeeds.

Oxycontin. "Take two and call me in the morning" has become "take two every hour for months and call me from jail."

Pfizer. Even despicable old white pricks who own six houses they've never been in and have maids they don't know the name of like to get all fucked up and drive their boats with their dicks - they just don't like giving their drug money to the Blacks or the Hispanics.

Queen's Grandson. Like all gingers, Prince Harry is a caner of grandiose proportions who likes nothing more than snorting a rock of coke as big as a babies fist and jerking off while he watches his polo ponies fuck.

Rock n Roll. Next time someone starts talking to you about the evil of drugs and how terrible they are for society just start screaming "Sympathy for Devil" at them and doing some baddass air guitar.

Sleep. What's the best thing about crystal meth? Only two sleeps 'til Christmas.

Teeth. If you eat through your nose, veins or lungs long enough your teeth just

kind of say, "Okay well I can see we aren't wanted here" and dissolve.

Urine Sample. A clean urine sample may be the only good reason to not abort that baby your dealer / boyfriend chucked up your brat-motel.

Vowel. E or ecstasy is a brilliant drug that makes the taker feel totally fucking awesome. The clue to its staggeringly good effect is in the name. The first people to take it didn't look at each other and say - "I like it - let's call it 'Quite Good'.

Wrap Star. You can tell a lot about your dealer by the way their wraps look.
The one that's made from Lottery tickets: If that's not screaming out at you that you are basically taking a huge gamble and the chances of you actually buying cocaine are about 1 in 129,008,009,000 then I don't know what is.
The ones that come in the covers of glossy woman's mags: Go round to a girls house and see a stack of coverless Marie Claires and you know you are looking at a prime time strawberry. This is a girl who watches her man fold his deals up and, waits for him to finish and rubs her gums all over

the coffee table while she sobs and masturbates at the same time. The sound of ripping paper elicits a Pavlovian saliva response and her pupils dilate like when you bring a North Korean political prisoner out of solitary into the light.

The messy ones: That dude is taking key-bumps out of all the wraps as he drives around in his rented Golf. He deals because it's the only way he can pay for his shit. Look in the car - are there food wrappers on the floor? No. That's because the last meal he ate was last Wednesday at 4pm and it was a finger dipped in a Nutella jar. The other reason those wraps look like a Cerebral Palsy art student folded them is because the dudes hands are shaking like a black and white minstrels hands at the end of a song.

The Russian Origami master: The neat, nicely folded, perfectly square envelopes that look like the symbol for email you see online. These guys drive cars leased under their mothers name that have baby seats in the back, even though they don't have kids - they use kids to sharpen their knives on.

These dudes are mostly Eastern Bloc and have lost a close family member to radiation or old age... 45-years-old. Don't ask for credit cos credit dismembers. The stuff is shite BTW. Perfectly white shite - the BNP of the drug world.

The plastic bag: At least you can see what you are not getting. I'd like to say that these guys are more honest than the wrappers... The one benefit about the plastic bag is that your coke won't get wet when you drop it on the piss-swamp of a floor in the shit-hole club (if you're under 30) or pub (if you're over 30). And another is you can, at a glance, see how long it's going to be before you have to duck out to the ATM and make that embarrassing call to the guy to come back to meet you a second time. They are like hour-glasses of doom.

Xenon Gas. This gas is used in flash lamps and arc lamps and as an anesthetic. Meaning it's used to melt metal and the minds of the hippy chemists who can make it in their basements.

"**Y**es" When you're on drugs everything is a good idea especially the idea of "let's get more drugs." That's the best idea ever.

Zip Lock. General rule: If you are buying your drugs in a zip lock freezer bag you have a problem with drugs.

Many soldiers are coming home from war missing the combat. They miss the war. They miss the sense of brotherhood and purpose that war gives them. They feel close to their fellow grunts. They talk of it being something real. It speaks volumes about our society that people return from war to the shopping malls and TV and superficial friendships that we all prefer as we retreat into screens and slowly wean ourselves off other human beings that they want to return to a place where their life is a danger. We have always had war and we'll always be at war and believing anything else is naive and frankly stupid especially as what we are supposed to be fighting for becomes ~~something~~ something we'd rather run away from.

AK47. - You can always tell the bad guys in movies because they are holding the AK47s. But in actual fact the AK is the gun of the people and responsible for the liberation of many oppressed minorities... IE: people that aren't Americans.

Butt Naked (General). There's always some part of Africa that's in the middle of a war and they're always fought over diamonds by the craziest, human heart-eating, impervious to bullet claiming, child-soldier using, baby-raping bunch of machete-wielding, tuxedo-pant-wearing, jewellery-made of-genital adorned, drugged up murderers there are. Which I kind of like. At least there's a sort of honesty to their brutality that our warlords try to deny and hide. I think we would all feel a lot better if Obama announced a troop surge wearing a necklace made of the dicks of his enemies and flanked by 9 year-olds drunk on whiskey, high on PCP and licking the sharp edges of their hunting knives.

Colonialism. In the old days war used to be clearcut. Someone had some shit you wanted and they looked weaker than you so you got your guys and whatever killing tools you had and went over to them and took their shit and made it your shit. You have guns they have sticks. Their shit is now your shit. Then you'd move some of your people in to run the place for a while and eventually, when you'd pulled enough shit out of their country and got enough of your people rich you'd leave. But that was the good old days - you know, 2007.

Draft. The draft is what happens when a government declares war and the people have to go and fight it. Surprisingly, not everyone wants to go to fight a war and kill other people so the government instates a draft and says either got to war and go to jail. To make it 'fair' the draft is done by lottery - but like all lotteries it's really only the poor that seem to play week after week.

Evil. It's really that simple, guys. Some people are evil-doers and need to be stopped. Any questions? No. Good. Now let's get to it. Umm, send in the Blacks and Hispanics first.

Frappe'. It used to be the world was divided into sovereign things called countries. These countries were filled with things like wood and steel, wool and shit like lithium - 'resources'.

These resources belonged to the countries. The resources were the country's wealth and future and were worth fighting for. These countries were also blessed with history, art and culture which were also worth fighting for. But now culture is an homogenised beige paste made in corporate focus groups by the least artistic among us.

So now corporations own the resources and make the culture - we're all basically going to war and killing each other so Starbucks can open in Iran.

Glory. Ever been poor and then suddenly you become mates with a really rich guy? It's fucking awesome. It's exactly like the show Entourage. You get to hang out and do shit way above your station. You get to eat what Vinnie eats, drive around in his cars, sit on his couches and leave his beer cans in his Jacuzzi. Sometimes he'll say shit like, "These are your size - you want them?" And occasionally you'll get to fuck his cast offs. Okay once in a while you'll have to pick up his laundry and cop a nick name like Turtle but it's a lot better than chopping the heads of sheep at the local meat packing plant. The American military is exactly like that for the soldiers that join up. That big fat state teat that has unlimited budget for keeping America safe and keeping beer cold. Sure, lots of the money goes to upgrading the capabilities of submarines for the fight against ISIS and is syphoned off to the 'industrial' part of the complex but a big fat rich-guy-friend amount goes to running bases and that means bowling alleys, cinema complexes, shopping malls, housing and very socialist sending state paid for education. It's a damn site better than life outside the military for young Americans. And, depending which part of the Empire you're posted, all you have to do is *maybe* go to war and maybe shoot someone - (like that episode of Entourage where Turtle shot that blonde girl and chopped her up in the pool house after Vinnie had that bout of impotence). Glory on the battle field is no longer the prize - it's the cost.

Hitler. There are tonnes of evil bastards in the history books but when your despotic aspirations are hindered only by the logistical considerations of body disposal you're really in a league of your own.

In God We Trust. Wars make money. More to the point. Wars move money. Wars move money from the tax paying people to the arms making people, the security providing people, the reconstruction people and the people that make tee shirts that say support our troops. It's a pyramid scheme and like the construction of all pyramids, the bottom layer is dead, poor people. The real bitch of the bunch is that in the west we don't really need to fight. No one is lobbing rockets at us, invading us or putting us in shackles - an yet every decade or so our leaders pick up the guns, tanks and missiles and head off into the world and rob us blind.

Journalism. "We'll be right back with operation freedom talon hammer eagle hope freedom goodness hope freedom America freedom Justice after these messages from our sponsors." Tasteless. Morose. Morally corrupt.

Kill 'em all. Let God sort 'em out.

Lasers. More money is spent on the military than educashun, health, space exploration, and yet we still use small pellets of lead alloy to kill our foes and not dazzling blasts of light. Which leaves soldiers in the embarrassing position of having to make that "Bweeevvvfff, Bweeevffff!" noise every time they shoot their rifles.

Mercenary. If you like the idea of shooting a brown person but can't be bothered trying to conceal your crime and definitely aren't keen to do any time for murder why not join a private security company? You get a lanyard and an M16 and you can shoot as many brown people as you like as long as you fill in a PPUI6678 form afterwards and their holding a mop handle or wearing a school bag or talking on the phone.

Nuclear Codes. It's not a special suitcase that comes into the president's office and needs to be unlocked by three people all turning the key at the same time, and then some big black dude who the President calls Admiral says, "Sir you have no choice." And then they all unlock the cases together and someone says, "God help us all. Every one." It's some half asleep Russian kid who pushes the button because some short-circuiting blinking light on a control panel that was installed in 1987 told him to… God help us all. Every one.

Orders. Following orders is a must for war to be successful and to keep those who actually inflict the war on each other sane. If you follow orders you can remove your ability for independent thought. "I'm just following orders." Your brain has been centralized. This way someone who sets fire to a village school or drops some nerve agent on refugees can still look himself in the mirror every morning while brushing his teeth without punching his own reflection in the mirror and opening up an artery with one of the mirrors shards.

Peace. They say fighting for peace is like fucking for virginity but it actually a little more like raping for virginity.

Quebec. Rambo could never have been Canadian. Because Canadian Rambo wouldn't have returned all fucked up from fighting some unjust war in Asia and PTSD'd the shit out some local sheriff's. Canadian Rambo would just be some guy taking photos of wildlife and boning up on his ice fishing skills.

Revolution. It used to be that every few years there'd be a nice cleansing revolution but we are at a point now where there will be no revolution. That used to be our only defense against the wealthy landlords and people-owners - the threat of an uprising. That we would storm their castles and keep coming and coming until they ran out of bullets and we could scythe off their perfumed heads, drink their cognac and hang their testicles from the mirrors of our pick-up trucks. However, these days we don't revolt. If we revolt we lose the chance of harvesting their crumbs. We've been sold the trickle down dream. Keep them up there and the wealth will trickle down to us. The fact is, the only people to experience the trickle down effect are the failed models Oligarchs piss on in return for Tiffany necklaces.

Sharpie. Draw a picture of the prophet Mohammed and discover the wacky Muslim sense of humour. They have none. This makes them the worst of all the crazy fools in robes. Imagine we're on a high street during the middle of the day. The only people that are on that high street at 12pm are the unemployable and the insane - now let's throw the religion lens on it. The barefoot man reading 'Cat In The Hat' to a pigeon is a Christian, the woman with the tinfoil wrapped around her head shaking some twigs and a coat hanger she's tied together with wool and twine is Mormon, the man gently rocking in a puddle of his own urine and drinking methylated spirits is a Christian, the one who thinks he's controlling the phasing of the traffic lights by blinking is the Hindu. But the one sitting in the back of the bus in a hoody with his hands balled up in fists growling "what the fuck are you looking at?" is the extremist Muslim. At least that's how it feels. The others are babbling nut-jobs but they aren't threatening you with violence. And when you're faced with the 'growling in the hoody' type of insane the best thing to do is look at the floor or get off the bus before it blows up.

Terrorist. Say you're a virus and you're doing your thing as a virus does. Breaking down red blood cells, multiplying, crippling immune systems and what-not because that's what you do. You're not evil. You just 'do-you' like that. Then all of a sudden a God-damn vaccine comes along and wipes you and your virus brethren out. You were just doing your thing but the 'host' didn't like your brand of 'you' so along come the vaccines and now you're all dead. In this scenario who is the terrorist? Is it the virus? The Vaccine or the Host? Exactly. None of the above because Israel dropped a bomb on your hospital and killed your last remaining doctors.

Unbiased. Neutrality is a Swiss word meaning 'morally void'.

Velcro. If you need a steady stream of 18 year-olds to volunteer to get maimed in the sand for their country's rich a really great tool for recruitment is some Navy Seals. They're real-life action heroes that kill real-life boogie men and get to wear really great gear.

Welcome Home. What's super annoying is when all your soldiers don't die in the war because when they don't die they come home and they often need to be looked after. Sometimes it means you have to buy special bags for them to shit into because their bowels were shot out. Or it might mean that they need to be taught to walk again because they lost their legs from an IED. Or maybe they need to be medicated for anxiety because they saw things happen to other human beings and did things to human beings that they can never unsee or undo. Yes, veterans are a stone cold bummer. However there is a ray of

CHROMOSOME

If I had to choose I'd probably still tick the box with 'DUDE' written next to it. Being a women is still basically dangerous and maybe it always will be. Men are still possessive, bullying, rapey pricks who abuse women, sell them, make them wear sheets over their heads and treat them as jerking off props. There's this low level threat that permeates everything when you're a woman and this dark cloud that women face everyday that men don't. The beauty industry and celebrity culture touches nearly every facet of life for women and peddles the notion that you're defective if you're not some mean 'hot' cunt. I feel for young women in their teenaged years - the years where, for most people, confidence alludes them and this is the time they become the most culturally sentient without the benefit of cynicism and hatred that comes from life showing you ~~that~~ what your place in it actually is.

Abortion. The saddest thing about abortion is that the babies being aborted would probably make the most interesting adults. Apart from the tragically awful cases of rape, we are losing the babies of the extremely ambitious or the women with too much lightning in their hearts (and enough honesty and integrity to admit it) to raise a kid at this moment. Instead the pro-life goons are not aborting nearly enough of their fetuses and therefore letting a bunch of boring, deluded, judgmental, ill informed, babies through the net to grow up into those punchable, placard-jockey adults that spend their time fucking with the rest of us.

Burkah. 9 out of 10 women will tell you that it's criminal the way Muslim women are forced to cover themselves because of some patriarchal, bronze aged religion. But then 9 out of 10 women will tell you that sometimes the burkah would be a nice option to have in the wardrobe because humidity and hair and holding water and fat-day and what-the-fuck-I'm-33-years-old-why-am-I still-getting-pimples?

Christian Grey. Women struggle tirelessly to break the shackles of the limited view men seem to have of their abilities intellectually and emotionally. Women not only have to be as good as their male counterparts but better than them to get the same level of respect. And over the years it feels like women are finally breaking though. Getting somewhere. Maybe an equal footing – at least in the way they are perceived... and then 100 million chicks buy 50 Shades of Grey and it's back to square one.

Duck Face. So the theory goes that lipstick is used to mimic the vagina when it's engorged. It subliminally excites men because men love a blood filled sex organ. I get that - but I promise you that no men are turned on by the face you're pulling in all your selfies. Your lips look less like a fun little vagina and more like a vagina that's done too much ketamine and can't stop drooling.

Eating. Guilt, shame, relationships, fear, worry, stress, love, doubt... These days, it seems, women eat everything but food.

Fankles. Give yourselves a break. What have your ankles done to deserve this derogatory term? All your ankles have ever done is be an elegant solution for connecting legs to feet (but maybe stay away from the strappy gladiator heels?)

Glass Ceiling. Sorry young lady, we don't have many management roles available for you I'm afraid. But pick up that glass cleaner and rag we could always use another cleaner. The glass ceiling is all streaked up with blood and hairspray from other women like you bashing their heads into it constantly for the past 50 years.

Having It All. This is a made up phrase by the media. What it means is that if you have worked your arse off and established yourself a career - you haven't got a family… and if you decided to have a family - you haven't got a career. But which ever terrible fucking life choice you made, buy our magazine because we have a glib article or the perfect outfit for the way out of this personality defect you're inflicting on the rest of us. Fuck you Gwyneth. Fuck you to hell.

"**I**NCRED" The relationship between gay men and straight women is a complicated one. Yes sometimes a gay man may keep a women as a pet so he can stand next to her and look thin but it's not all one way. Gay men also provide women with valuable opinions and insights on fashion, fierceness and helpful ways to shorten words to save valuable time that can be used for drinking white wine and ranking 1D in order of who would be best at oral sex.

Jokes. Some people say that women aren't funny. I'll just say there is no evolutionary imperative for women to be able to tell jokes - that's a man's burden. This is not to say that women aren't funny, it is to say that women aren't desperately trying to be like the future of the human race depends on it. The woman's imperative is to somehow forgive the constant barrage of spittle filled anecdotes and pitches that come at them every time they leave the house wearing anything but Ugg Boots.

"Kate" "Kate is walking for Givenchy again! How old is she now? Like 40?" You mean Kate Moss? You call her Kate? Stop calling people you don't know by their first names alone. It's desperate and creepy. Unless you can show me her number in your phone, use her full name. On second thoughts stop talking about people you don't know - it's boring and lame.

Listening. "Hearing is not listening, Dave. "

Mother Fucker. A woman's relationships with her father is important as it's the thing that keeps women from getting pole bruises on their inner thighs. It's a tricky balance of being hugged enough and not being hugged too, too much.

No Means No. Living in a world where 50% of the population is always thinking about what your boobs and wee-wee place look like must be really fucking exhausting.

Orgasm. Women didn't even have orgasms until the 1980's. Before that they just hosted men's orgasms in their genitals like damp convention centres made of velvet.

Premenstrual Syndrome Defence. Sometimes every single month you might want to stab your husband's stupid fat face into little chunks of flesh so small that looks like it was coughed out of a lung. And then one month you might actually do it. If that happens the police will turn up with their annoying sirens and dumb questions about your dead husband. At this point just stay calm(ish) and remember that Premenstrual syndrome defense is a thing. Premenstrual Syndrome Defense has been successfully pleaded as a criminal defense in Britain (IE: A jury of some very understanding peers mixed with a jury of some very scared shitless peers) and will be 100% more effective than what you were going to go with: "His face was all facey".

Queen B. One thing that Beyoncé has taught us all is that feminism is a lot more naked than it used to be.

Really? Really? Really? Men don't understand the way women talk because women actually communicate. Ask a question, wait for the answer, listen, understand, be empathetic, offer an opinion, connect - repeat. For men it's just a series of calling each other a cunt, talking about each others wife's tits and telling each other how their kid looks like he might be gay until one man breaks and has to leave.

Sciatica. The average handbag contains at least one computer, sunglasses options, enough make up to start a MAC pop-up store, a wallet filled with 451 loyalty cards from the same place all with one stamp on each of them, credit cards filled with lies, Hygienic wipes (for prozzie washes), three different hand sanitizers, mints, skittles, nurofen extra, tampons (back up tampons because I menstruate a lot), broken pen, a spoon, a toothbrush, expired coupons, a small tree's worth of receipts and at least a kilo of dust, skin flakes and fake eye hair - which is why the hand bag is as big as a sleeping bag and weighs as much as a Oprah's fridge.

Theobrama Cacao Seed. You know how we know crack cocaine is good? It's the only thing that stops women from eating chocolate.

Ugg Boots. The most effective feminist protest tool in the history of the struggle. Nothing says "I'm a lady who likes to fart. A lot." like a pair of Ugg Boots. Burning bras was a shitty idea. All that happened is men got to see womens' nipples. A mixed message at best. But wearing Uggs was a stroke of genius. It said: We're done wearing high heels and giving-a-shit for men. It said: We're going to walk around looking like we have the flu on the way to having multiple verrucas removed from our feet and we sometimes fart a lot because fuck your male imposed 'standards'.

Vagina. A woman's vagina is a scary and confronting thing. No man wants to see one cold. Not just HELLO VAGINA. If you want the truth we think they're freaky and remind us of the Predators mouth before it makes that clicking noise and fights Schwarzenegger. That's why boobs were invented. To warm men up for the viewing of the vagina. We see boobs and we start to get ready - basically it puts us on alert and our brains go into defcon pink.

Wrong. Women are never wrong. The worst they can ever be is not right.

X Husband. Women are now more likely to be murdered by someone they know than a stranger. It's statistically safer for a woman to knock on a random door and spend the night cuddled up to a man she doesn't know than it is to stay home and over cook a steak.

Yoga Pants. The science is back. This just in. Wearing yoga pants to drink coffee and eat cake on Sunday morning is as effective at making people you believe you go to yoga as actually going to yoga.

Zara. Okay so we all know that it's terrible how Bangladeshi kids sometimes get crushed under the crumbling concrete of collapsing clothing factories and it's terrible how the doors are found locked from the outside when fires claim the lives of 100's of garment workers and it's terrible that human rights abuses run rampant throughout the entire industry… but you know what isn't terrible? Runway looks without the runway prices - that shit is not terrible one bit.

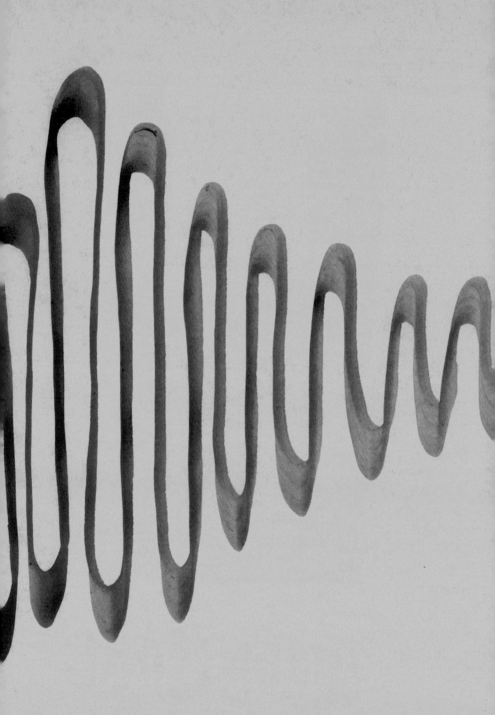

CHROMOSONE

Are you bored of you? If you are you're probably a man. Are you bored of watching sport on TV, drinking beer, calling Gay men faggots, scoring 'pussy', wanting a new car, wearing hats, growing that fuckin' beard, shaving it off, wishing you had bigger biceps, not being able to explain your feelings, liking music only made from people who look like you, reading magazines that rank watches, acting like you don't care, pretending you're not scared to death and shitting yourself the whole time, being cunty to women, feeling impotent and without purpose, following, being a half arsed father, knowing more about how some player feels about losing a trophy than knowing about how you yourself feel about your own apathy. Are you bored of you? If you are you're probably a man.

&

Abdominals. In the final step towards womanhood men now buy magazines with pictures of other men on them and have started feeling body image anxiety while seeking advice on how to 'blast their ab's' and 'get ripped in 80 seconds'. Listen Colin - you can't pick up an axe and chop some wood for a fire with your abs or feed your kids with them so don't covet them. Faggot.

Bachelor. Sure you can do what ever you want whenever you want. Sure you have 52inch televisions, a motorbike for casual occasions and one for formal situations, at least 4 pairs of really cool sunglasses (none of which make them look they're trying too hard), all your own hair, a guitar that was won in a poker game from legend of the blues legend Bobby 'Mud Fish' Ranks, some sketches for this art thing you're working on and a phone that won't stop beeping with opportunities of the flesh... But are you free? Is that what you are? Time to take a good hard look at yourself and this bad-boy boots 'n' denim life you think you're living. Maybe not as cool and interesting as you like to tell yourself you are as you masturbate in the mirror and growl at your own reflection. May-be underneath the facial hair, half recorded acoustic-rap albums and complicated handshakes you share with various bouncers around town you're just a scared little momma's boy sleeping on dirty sheets. Ouch. The truth hurts. Ding-a-ling it's wake up time. It's time to realize that the whole world thinks you are a loser and whether you like it or not, as a bachelor, you exist other people's eyes. No matter how hard you tell yourself that you are a loner - you're not. You're just alone. No matter how many times you say you don't care what other people think - you do. And now you can add 'deluded' to your list of deplorable personality traits. The truth is you are desperate for us married guys with the 'adorable' kids to give you our approval. You only exist because we say you do. You are a tree falling in the forest that only makes a noise because we love watching you fall. We are watching and we are laughing our arses off. Ha ha fucking ha ha! (PS: can you email us some of the photos of your latest threesome on the back of that yacht on a Wednesday with chicks you instantly forgot the names of - that'd be sweet.)

Comet. When you're bald and you also have a ponytail that hairstyle is called 'The Comet'. So named because your forehead looks like a shining space rock with a hair tail streaking behind it as you strut through a nightclub carrying the Smirnoff Ices you just bought for the three girls who are unsuccessfully looking in their purses for a flying-fuck to give that you're "back into music again" and doing some "groovy" demos in your home studio.

Dude. "Dude? Dude! Du-uuuudde… Dude, dude, dude." Perfect man-conversation over.

Evisceration. 'Life intervention' by wild animal isn't as common as it once was because men are no longer men. Men are basically just women who stand up when they pee-pee. It used to be that a man would fight an animal with a sharp stick and more often than not sustain an injury that would probably kill him. It was honorable and left a decent legacy. Now we live until we 100 and our legacy is the filth on our Google search history.

Fighting. Friday nights in most drinking precincts in the world will be your hotspot for fights. Basically anywhere with booze, men and women. Normally it starts with a rival man looking at someone's woman and ends with punches being thrown, and shirts being torn, all to the soundtrack of the dumb blonde who started it screaming, "Leave him Kevin - he's not worth it."

Guitar. "I'm a cowboy. On a steel horse I ride. I'm wanted. Dead or alive." … You're not, Craig. You're a manager of a plumbing supplies store, you're still 9 payments away from owning your 2002 Toyota Camry outright and you have gout.

Heterosexual. Being heterosexual is fucking gay. Having sex with a woman is easy - fucking a dude hurts. It's way more heterosexual to be gay than it is to be heterosexual. If it were a choice like the religious right suggests it is - then all dudes would choose gayness. Easy fucking choice especially if you like fun and things that are awesome. Gay dudes are slowly taking all best things and making them theirs. Neatness. Fitness. Beards. Unprotected sex with strangers. The word 'fist'. The word 'Gay'.

Convertibles. Dancing well. Singing Aretha Franklin songs into a hairbrush. Eating a banana in public. Eating a banana on your knees. Appreciating a rainbow. Hard hats and tool belts - all over this nation dudes are risking severe head trauma because every time they don a hard-hat with a tool belt they are worried that the Indian and the Cop and the Sailor are going to turn up. Leaving us with ill fitting jeans and... Maroon 5. Because homosexual men in their 20's and 30's are the most fun-having human beings on the planet - only rivaled by the sons of Mexican cocaine cartel bosses who carry gold guns and keep human beings as pets. Do you know how rich you have to be to pull that shit off as a straight dude? Cocaine cartel rich - that's how rich. But ANY 24-year-old homo can have a chubby human women as a pet! They're called Fag-hags and they'll follow him around wherever he goes whenever he wants and even buy him his drinks. Some hetero dudes are scared to death of gays. Because? They're scared they'll become gay? And you can't catch Gayness (if you could I'd be licking the toilet seat in bars). You can catch H.I.V but not Gayness. So relax, Bigot - you're probably not going to become gay. But here are some precau-

tions you can take to make sure. Say you are sucking a man's cock IF you hum the theme tune to Monday Night Football - that's not gay. It's not gay to make love to a man... IF YOU WIN! It's not gay make out with a guy and give him a hand job - If you are wearing your wife's clothes and make up. Keep that in mind.

Intimacy. Forget herpes or gonorrhoea, intimacy is the STD most men fear most.

Jenna Jameson. A quick hint: It's not cool to have a favorite pornstar, dudes.

Kinky. Not a word of a lie if the average woman knew what the average man wanted to do, on, near and because of her body she'd be sick into her hands... which the average man wouldn't mind... not one... little... bit.

Lycra. It used to be about buying a Harley Davidson and a leather jacket and giving the finger to the world... But now men buy an expensive bicycle, stuff themselves into Lycra and set about doing the world's slowest victory lap in the Tour De Farce.

Mid Life Crisis. The reason you are not Brad Pitt or the lead singer of that band-you-don't-know the-name-of-but-your-daughter's-friends-like has nothing to do with the fact you are a talent free zone and everything to do with the fact you're being stifled by your negative wife, unimaginative friends, domineering boss and your selfish newborn. They are holding you back, dude. Time to ditch the dead weight and get radical (lonely). Okay so your mate's wives won't be your biggest fans. You represent a virus that could infect their lame-ass husbands too. They will call you "pathetic" and your mates will agree that yes, you are pathetic (even though they think you're actually a baddass and your new GoPro quad copter mount is SICK!) The thing about your new life you need to remember is 'Wednesdays'. On the weekends you're a 'cool older guy doing the weed and buying the drinks with a great new car and Cialis in his pocket' but on Wednesday you're just a fat bloke with frosted tips and credit card debt thumbing through stand-up paddleboard catalogues and wondering if waxing your chest would make your moobs look more svelte while eating tuna out of a can and wishing you could see your dog (and maybe kids).

Negging. BOOM - you're a woman and you're minding your own business and one day some prick walks into a room and you immediately know, "That guy is a prick." You look at him and everything about the prick makes you want to attack his head with the blunt end of a cricket stump and then chip his genitals off with the sharp end so you leave the room so don't end up doing time for murder. And if you didn't absolutely know from looking at the prick there's a chance that he'll walk up to you and say something like - "nice handbag, people who buy the real ones are just silly. So well done on the fake". Negging. This prick is from breed of men called PUA's or Pick Up Artists who employee cheap tactics and psychological tricks to fool women into fucking them. The leaders of this band of fucktards are a bunch of creepy nerdlings who have goatees like out of work magicians, masturbate in the mirror and wear David Beckhams cologne while practicing 'approaches' and they make us all nostalgic for when date rapists would just use Rohypnol or get jobs as cab drivers.

Outdoors. North Face mountaineering gear is the uniform of middle-aged surrender. Men treat Gore-Tex like it's some magic Harry Potter cloak that they'll drape over themselves and adventures will happen. Men also think that women are impressed by this technical outer apparel. Women are not impressed by 'moisture wicking' fabrics. They think men who dress like pole explorers while ordering a latte look like over cautious toddler who fucks with his socks on – and it grosses them out it makes their vaginas dry… like their panties are made with North Face moisture wick technology.

Pointless. These days men don't really build anything. There are no wild beasts to slay. Kids can be made in a lab and our penises don't vibrate at three different speeds. Men are just dumb relics from a bygone era. Like a lost animal desperately trying to be relevant by creating dramas, conflicts and sports so they have something to do that seems important, when really the gig has been up for 40 years. We get dressed in a costume of some sort and climb into our cars and screech off to some arbitrary building where we all furrow our brows and point at things and yell cool shit like, "I don't care, Jen-

kins. Just get it done or it'll be curtains for you." And then Jenkins shits himself and gets all worked up about the impending 'curtains' and low and behold we've created some façade of purpose for a little while longer. War, religion, banking, engines, gadgets, honor, golf. All of it is just shit made up by men to keep ourselves busy and to stop us from killing our families with a knife and then swallowing some buckshot with a blank face and a shrug.

Qyying. "Oh what's wong? Are those tears? Are you qyying? " Today we ask the question, "Is it okay for a man to cry?" The answer is, of course, not really. Something happens when a man cries – a kind of pathetic aura emanates from the very core of their man-ness causing confusion and unpleasantness to anyone in the surrounding space like a tear gas canister dropped into a kindergarten at nap time. When one sees a man crying it's hard to know what to do. Does one comfort him and hold him while he sobs? Or does one throw a blanket over him and beat him around the torso with a bible in pillowcase? I don't have the answer to this question because I just run. I run hard and fast until my lungs burn and my mouth tastes like copper coins.

Razor. Here are the scientific facts about beards - and who are you to argue with science? Fact 1: If you are a man and don't have some sort of hair on your grill, you are indistinguishable from a woman or a child. Fact 2: A man with a smooth face is a repellent abominat because men who have beards are superior lovers. Fact 4: Beards were born in the fires of Valhalla and forged with Thor's mighty hammer. This is man's natural state. If 'big razor' hadn't been lobbying us so hard for so many years, appealing to our gadget genes by adding blade after blade to their razors and thus making it irresistible to shave, all men would sport a full beard - and sport it hard because what it says about you is undeniable: That you can skin a rabbit, tie a knot, park a boat, shake a hand, punch a bully, climb a cliff, evade capture, laugh at danger, talk to a dolphin, extinguish a fire and make love to a woman while in a plummeting airplane. In short: You are a man. There are other options for a male if the full beard is not what you're looking for. There's the handlebar Moustache AKA Prison Tache: Although not strictly a beard, this is a favorite style for any man who needs to toughen up his look. It basically makes you look like a total fucking badass who has done some time in the big house and who won't hesitate to pop a punks eye out of his snitching skull and replace that eye with his own dick. There's also the straight up Mo. When you are dealing with a man who has chosen the path of the lone moustache you are dealing with a no nonsense hombre. It takes integrity and bravery to wear face hair solely on the top lip and you can be sure that anything the moustache owner says will be the Goddamned truth not some Communist jibber jabber you might hear from a bald faced pinko. This is a man who wants the world to know that his sock drawer is ordered and his Hi-Fidelity sound system is German. But never under any circumstance head towards the goatee. Unless you're a Mexican hit man, the goatee is a nerd beard. All it says about you is that under your ankle length leather coat you wear a cellphone on a belt clip and have a vast knowledge of the hidden backstory of the Matrix trilogy.

Strippers. This is your best hope of having butt sex. Most strippers have Daddy issues. They've either not been hugged enough... or hugged way too much. All you have to do is slide on in there and say something like, "I'm so proud of you. Look you can get you ankles all the way to your ears. I'm very, very proud of you." And get ready - you might want to use some hand sanitiser as lube.

Trilbys. **And Tattoos** Every king needs a crown and ours is the trilby. The trucker hat is too done - even you know that... now. Besides the jaunty, semi-formal trilby matches our new dangerous skull tattoo. We are now the complete sex-package. It's like Humphrey Bogart meets a Hells Angels cool biker dude... and then goes to bed at 10pm after Top Gear and Haagen Das.

Urethra. Dear Milkers, There's a polite way to piss in a public toilet and it involves not making eye contact with the dude next to you, not whistling the Frozen theme song and , most importantly, shaking your dick at the end of your piss NOT MILKING IT FREE OF EXCESS URINE. What the fuck? You dudes who finish your piss and then squeeze up and down your shaft like your piss is a viscous snake venom and needs to be cajoled out IT DOESN'T the piss is out of the pipe already - it's not stuck there waiting for a massage from your nasty little fingers. There are just a couple of dew drops on the tip there's not magic fun-fluid in your balls that needs to be lovingly caressed to the surface. You're milking it you dick milker! Why are you milking it? Just give your dick a quick shake and put it away. Shake and away. Don't stand there next to us giving yourself a flacid wank. You come across like a creepy out of work magician with a goatee and full length leather coat.

Thanks,
Shakers

VeeJay. Okay. Listen to me. Look at me. Listen to me and look at me. VeeJays are not role models you fucking idiots. Say it with me. "VeeJays are what? Not role models." That's good. Now take off the BEATS headphones and go and raise your kids.

Wank. When a man wanks it's a brutal and horrible act. It's more akin to an act of rage fuelled violence than an act of loving sex. Men treat their penises like American agents treat a Pakistani detainee at a

CIA black site in Yemen. The penis suffers extraordinary rendition from it's trouser home, is forced to look at some needlessly graphic images and then is beaten around the head until it throws up all over the floor. Never truly understanding why and never knowing when the next terrifying episode may take place. Even at the best of times that orgy of violence is hard to reconcile for the average man but with no clear motivation except boredom this act becomes a small death of everything decent inside him and a walk towards the dark truth that men, every man, is totally fucking pointless. And the worst? The boredom wank. The worst of all wanks. It's an empty and soulless pursuit that leaves the practitioner ejaculating, not just a puddle of tepid child soup, but part of his very soul. Too many boredom wanks and a man becomes a monster with nothing but hollow hatred behind his eyes - look at Pope Francis for example. Truly chilling.

X-Men. Comic books and movies are for kids. If you're a grown man who still goes to these movies fantasizing about your super mutant power may I suggest you probably have one - it's the ability to make people laugh their arses off as soon as you turn your back. May I be so bold as to suggest your mutant name? Virgin Man.

"**Y**ou Lucky Cunt" Topping every man's wish list is a threesome. Sorry, every hetero man's wish list - for Gay dudes 'ménage a trios' is French for Wednesday. Sorry one more amend, a GIRL, GIRL, GUY threesome the other is gay by proxy and you should just come out and fill your mouth with a dick and stop using that poor girl to get some dudes cum on your skin. Now - have you ever tried to pat three dogs at one time?

Zipper. Why are you walking around with no underwear on under your jeans? It's not cool. It's creepy. Dudes who free ball have jeans so full of pubes and dick skin that the denim has rubbed off when they walk It's like a rattle snake nursery in there with all the shedding. Not to mention the farticles and skid marks that infiltrate the denim. You think you're cool and artistic don't you, dude? But you're not unless you count making Jackson Poo-locks in your Levis seats. You're a stinky denimed germ factory and deserve to lose the top inch of your knob every time you do your fly up.

ZOMBIE APOCALYPSE

As long as it happens to everyone I'm fine with it. As long as the whole world is plunged into chaos all at once I'm more than fine with it. I actually sort of look forward to it. It's like a divorce. There's a bit of pain up front and you might lose your kids and have to live in your car but you get to hang out with your friends a lot and you never have to change your pants.

Anarchy. Don't think of it as the end of the world. Think of it as the start of your freedom. No more work, no more gym membership, no more opinions, no more gluten free, no more drinks with the client. Just glorious screaming looting, killing, gang naming, fire worshipping and living by your wits. Anarchy is like summer camp for people who don't mind the sight of blood.

Bolts. Bullets can only be fired once but crossbow bolts can be discharged many, many times. I plan on doing quite a bit of killing during the Apocalypse so the Crossbow will be my weapon of choice. So much so that I have sewed little sponges under the arms of my leather Apocalypse jacket for wiping the people-blood off my precious bolts.

Cars. Apocalypse cars are amazing. Bladed, super-charged, covered in bones, filthy and forever bouncing raider off the bonnets. The only problem with them is that they're all 1980's muscle cars and will take a lot of petrol to run leaving you in constant crossbow battles with feather wearing lunatics over the nuclear wastelands of our dead cities… But fuck it. Worth it. MadMax would never have survived if he was the sort of soft-cocked-mary who owned a Prius.

Day 2. Day one of an apocalypse will be fine. A little unsettling but mostly just making shadow puppets on the wall with your flashlights during the blackout. Day two on the other hand… Work out what you'll be keen to sell your kids for now. It'll save precious moments in the knifepoint negotiation that will take place at around 6pm.

Equality. The cause of most of the unhappiness and anxiety in the world is the relative position we hold within society. It's never - "how am I doing?" It's always "How am I doing compared to that guy?" What the tumbling towers of chrome and glass signify is not just 'no more meetings' it also means that we are all the same finally. All just lice infested beings wearing CROCS as a hat picking through the memories of civilization for scraps.

Forrest. Run.

Gold. You mean that soft yellow metal that you can't make arrowheads with? Fuck off, mate I'm not trading my tarpaulin for no soft gold that won't hold an edge and won't cut off the ears of a corpse. Now piss off before you get raped and eaten by me the feared and baby-blood covered 'Gasoline Reaper!'.

Hedge Fund Manager. This is what you'll order at roadside meat outlets. You'll come in and say, "Do you have any Hedge Fund Manager?" and the butcher will say, "Why, yes. A pack of raping murderers bought some in this morning freshly raped and murdered." And then you'll swap a liter of petrol you siphoned out of an abandoned tank for a pectoral and an arm with a Rolex still on it.

"**I** Told You So" All the religions will try and take credit for the plague of death that has been afflicted upon humanity by saying it was foretold in their particular book. That's the moment to break out the slow clap as you approach their houses of worship with lit torches and hardons.

Jake The Snake Roberts. The people best prepared for the coming end of days are professional wrestlers. They are strong, violent, their costumes are generally torn up tee-shirts and badd-ass death-leather and their stage names are the type we'll all end up giving our-selves because Warren Jen-kins won't put fear into the heart of anyone - especially not some dude who just named himself 'Gasoline Reaper'.

Keith Richards. Look for him and do what ever he does. That dude cannot die and will be sitting on a velvet cushion in the only clean room in the world giving cockroaches survival tips

Leather Pants. It might be a good idea to start dress-ing like you will never be able to change clothes again. Like these are the last clothes you will ever wear and hope like fuck that the apocalypse doesn't hap-pen while you are at a cos-tume party or going to job interview or in a boy band. You always see dudes in suits in End of Days films and they are the first to die. I would also steer away from tee shirt with jokes or slogans on them. That tee shirt with I FUCK ON THE FIRST DATE, although hilar-ious now will get old fast (and won't help you with the rape brigades that will pa-trol the streets with hard-ons and tire irons).

Meeting. What do we do now that could transfer into a semi decent skill set af-ter the Apocalypse? All we do is send emails and have meetings about the email or, even better, a meeting about an upcoming meeting or the meeting just passed. A meet-ing about a meeting about an email. I myself am fucking useless. I feel a real, honest and visceral sense of accomplishment if I piss someone else's skidmarks off a toilet bowl.

Night. Probably best you leave nighttime to the tough bastards. You're good to scramble around the rubble looking for a can of Fanta someone else might have missed and trading in sparrows eggs for from the hours of 5am to 7pm while the night raiders sleep off their killing frenzy.

Office Supplies. The only unlooted stores in all the cities will be the stores that sell A4 printer paper, post-it notes and ergonomic office chairs. While you'll be able to swap a sharpened pool cue for a tin of tuna in most cities, a case of yellow highlighters won't even get you some mushed up cockroach paste in a bread bag.

Prepper Pussy. 'Preppers' are people that have been preparing for the apocalypse for a long time. There are an estimated 3 million in the USA alone. They have years worth food, water and big guns hidden in their military grade bunkers. 'Prepper Pussy' is what you will have to become to get into their bunker and avoid the raping cannibal hordes.

Quiff. The way we look won't matter like it didn't matter in the old days - all that time we spend on our hair we get back. We would smash mirrors and use the shards as daggers for cutting venison and for arrowheads. Our hair will grow long and we'd all have dirty clothes and beards. We'd basically look like a that guy in IT that leaves finger prints on our keyboards when he comes to change your email settings after the server shits itself.

Raping Hordes. Raping is the go-to method of handling any and all disaster situations these days. Any war zone - raping. Afghanistan - raping (except the women there don't notice the difference, as that has pretty much been stock standard for 1000 years). Airline crash - raping. I bet the whole eating people on the freezing mountaintop after the plane crash thing was not out of hunger but out of an attempt to destroy raping evidence. It's like raping is just under the surface with everyone and as soon as no one is looking and there are no 'parents; watching - raping! What happened to jumping on the bed and eating ice cream for dinner?

Stranger. A stranger is just a person that hasn't raped you yet.

Toe Nail. After the dental floss factories become homes for 'The Disciples Of The New Lord' and the tooth picks are all used in bird traps a TOP TIP to remember is the big toenail is the best toenail to use as a tool to get rat meat out of your teeth.

University Degree. The varnished oak frame on your Business Commerce degree will make excellent kindling as the varnish will burn hot and fierce. The fine, thick cartridge paper it's printed on will work well to blot up the blood from your latest stab / bite / rape wound too… so totally worth getting.

Vengeance. Forgiving and forgetting was for before the flames. If you're someone's boss now pray you never ever run into them after the ash starts raining - they might want to give you a performance review with a brick tied to kettle cord.

Wah! Wah! Wah! There has been very little turmoil in the lives of white people and so when the rules of society that white people wrap around them like a security blanket disappear they're not going to handle it well at all. If I were white I'd start practicing begging for my life now.

X On Doors. As you wander the dying earth with your necklace made of children's ribs wearing two different shoes and carrying a table leg wrapped in barbed wire as your only defense you'll need a bit of shelter at night to escape the 'Young-uns'. Personally I think ignore the warnings and do go into the houses with the red X's on the doors. You'll either get some sleep or get 'the sickness' either one is a win at this point.

Yonkers, NY. Of course, there are some places on the planet where they won't even notice the fucking difference.

Zoo Escapees. The big cats, angry baboon troupes and remaining polar bears that will inevitably roaming the city streets should be motivation enough for you to start putting down the doughnuts and picking up the running shoes now. When the wolves start howling from the roof of the Wal-Mart - any fat fucks trying to get back to their makeshift shelter in the abandoned tyre yard aint gonna make it.